The Resilience of Being

An Anthology for Wherever You are on Your
Timeline

Edited by

Emma Willingham

ISBN: 978-1-9164916-1-8

DEDICATION AND THANKS

I would like to dedicate this book to my backers. Without their incredible support I wouldn't have been able to bring this project to life. So, *thank you* to:

Krisztina Bana, Jess Beedle, Ciara Boardman, Chris Brennan, James Brooke, Sophi Brown, Simon Buckley, Will Cass, Jenny Chester, Coco Oya CiennaRey, Moya Clark, Victoria Coffey, The Creative Fund, Emily Duff, Katie Falkner, Stephanie Ford, Nigel Garnett, Jenny Hill, Maria Hyde, Izzy Jones, Jenny Jones, Claudia Knight, the ladies of Long Preston WI, Adam Lawson, Emma Leverton, Catherine McAteer, Charlotte McSharry, Jacob Miller, Emily Mitchelson, Carys Morley, Aidan Morrison, Joe Paterson, James Pearson, Sonja Pretis, Beth Roberts, Esmè Smithson, Emily Stirk, Glen Taylor, George Watson, Stephen Willingham, Jonathan Willingham, June Willingham, Robert Willingham, Sally Windle and Ellie Wright.

I would also like to give great thanks to the authors in this anthology who have been brave and caring enough to allow me to share their stories.

Finally, thanks to the artists who have contributed to this anthology. With a distinct lack of artistic skill myself, I am so grateful to have the opportunity to showcase theirs:

Jacob Walden for the cover design
Libby Phillips for the author illustrations
'Amateur Magician' for the final thoughts image

FRONT COVER DESIGN

The front cover design was created by Jacob Walden.
Jacob is a 16-year-old artist living in Warwickshire. Having experimented with a variety of artistic styles, he utilises both digital and traditional art. His subjects include his friends, his family and the people he admires. He is going on to study Art at A-Level and he hopes to pursue a career in art in the future.
You can find more of Jacob's work on his Instagram:
@jacob.ben13

From the artist:
"For the cover of *The Resilience of Being*, I wanted to highlight the beauty found in all different body types. Slowly, our perception of beauty in society is changing to be more inclusive, and I wanted to show that through the illustration. Hopefully every reader will find an aspect of themselves within it. I also wanted to include the symbolism of the sunflowers. The sunflowers turn towards the sun in order to grow and flourish, just like we need to turn toward the positive things in life to keep going and to live well. Overall, I want people to see the cover and know that no matter what your insecurities are, over your physical appearance, you should be confident, because you are loved, and you are beautiful."

CONTENTS

For Anja and Amiena,

Published at last.

Lots of love,
    Sarah

Introduction
Emma Willingham, age 24

I started *The Resilience of Being* as a project to challenge the idea that our bodies exist just to be fixed. I want people to know that damaging ways of treating yourself do not need to be the default, even if you've gotten used to them by now.

Putting it rather bluntly, this project was created by someone whose fears around not being enough led to becoming overly friendly with negative, self-destructive behaviour. To save you a few years of catching up, I came to the quite startling realisation that punishing myself wasn't working to help me achieve any sort of peace or happiness.

It turns out, you can't hate yourself into loving yourself. So, perhaps it's time to try something else.

Body image is a concept that got under my skin and sat there and stewed for a while before I properly noticed it. I could see expressions of pointless self-criticism from everyone around me; they weren't necessarily cries for help, but simply normalised results of the daily scrutiny we place ourselves under.

Feeling out and recognising my own experiences with my body, the positive and the negative, brought to light how much I had been ignoring in my own behaviour. Then, seeing those I love dislike themselves so openly, I struggled with not being able to do anything to help. They were convinced there was something wrong with them, all because of whispered notions of how we are meant to act in order to feel worthy of respect. This was my boiling point: I had to talk about this. This was something to get angry about.

When coming around to challenging that outlook, you're likely to run headfirst into the world of body positivity and self-love. Wonderful ideals, but also incredibly daunting goals. It is not unusual to be overwhelmed by the idea of loving all parts of yourself. It jumps over the first step: how to accept your body as it is, and how to liberate yourself from the idea that your body equates to your worth as a person.

My progress has leapt and dipped throughout the year of this book being put together. Editing an anthology on body image really does make you look yourself in the eye. I am still learning, but one thing I am confident about is that immediately deciding to love yourself is not the only alternative; not hating yourself is a start. Self-love doesn't have to be about worshipping the way you look, but instead treating yourself with kindness in place of punishment.

This applies to everyone. *The Resilience of Being* is here to draw attention to the misconception that these body image pressures do not disappear and should not be dismissed in later stages of life. You will notice the age at time of writing for each author has been included with their story; this is a reminder that you can begin to question how you think about yourself no matter where you are at in your life.

In all honesty, I didn't know what this project was going to be at the start. I knew I felt close to this topic and had a lot mental energy surrounding it. I felt like my experiences had progressed enough for me to feel comfortable speaking about them and I thought I knew what needed to be said.

Since I have a penchant for words, the idea started as a blog post series. Then grew into an insert for a community newsletter. Then I attended a reading, for a book on women and equality, and body image popped up amongst other topics. At the end, I found myself making my way to the author, asking for her advice with my signature hesitancy. She told me that, ultimately, it is no good sending out the occasional tweet; you need to do more than just pressing buttons. This struck a chord with me, so I wanted to make this a wider conversation and see what I was missing.

When you think you know something, go talk to people about it. Learn as much as you can about it. Create discussion and hear points of view that never crossed your mind. Listen to stories that you will never be able to relate to. And then see what you can do about it.

I knew this needed to be a project made up of several different voices and I have been lucky enough to be able to capture some. Now, we're here with a collection of twenty experiences from a brilliant, diverse range of writers in a book that can be shared and used to help us dig our elbows in.

We have stories about the physical relationship with the body, tales on how others' possession can be imprinted on the body, stories about body image affecting your place in a community, experiences that have allowed people to find who they are meant to be in this life. We have stories of hope, struggle, discovery, growth, power, peace, exploration, and above all, honesty.

I cannot thank the contributors enough for their submissions; I have been touched by all these pieces. They have reminded me there is great strength in vulnerability, and that what you may view as 'giving up' is in fact just taking a pause, as there is always the option to carry on.

Which brings me to resilience. Resilience is the capacity to recover from difficulties and continue on. Sometimes, resilience looks like smiling through gritted teeth and putting all your energy into executing your day seamlessly. Sometimes, resilience looks like breaking down and letting yourself take time to weather the rough patch. And both of these are fine.

If I want you to take anything away from this, it is that the resilience of being is unique for everyone. To compare it is not helpful. While battling negative thoughts and behaviours is a struggle that can last a while, so will the person fighting them.

Whether you have this book for yourself, for someone you love, or simply out of human curiosity, thank you for taking the time to read. I hope it opens your eyes and lets you shout a little louder.

Dear Body
Bethany Rose, age 25

We have now spent twenty-five years together. And I owe you an apology.
I think it's time we talked.

You do get too much attention sometimes. Especially the 30Es and the height that's way under the 5 foot three that society sees as petite.

People comment on you, a lot, and I'm sorry that I don't fight back enough. But if I'm going to talk about acceptance, if I'm going to allow you to be vulnerable, to not be ashamed of you, I may as well do this properly.

I am sorry for the times
I let you be used
And the times you were bruised.
I am sorry for every time that I sliced you open.
I am sorry for allowing the girls at school
To comment on what you were
And what you weren't.

I am sorry for resenting you.
I am sorry for the exhausting hours I make you work, the sleep I

deprive you of, the rest you so desperately need.

I'm sorry for the years of weigh-ins not lie-ins that I've put you through.

I am sorry for not screaming loud enough when he hurt you. I know it isn't what you wanted because it isn't what I wanted either. I am sorry for what he forced us to do. He may have made us a victim, but we made ourself a survivor.

Skin.
I am sorry for the times I've torn you apart.
I am sorry for all the times you've sewn yourself back together.
I am sorry for the destruction I've put you through.
I am sorry for the layers of make-up I cover you with. The creams and colours that society deems are appropriate to be seen in public.

I'm sorry for the times I deprived you of dinner because I wished you could be thinner.

Skin.
Thank you for every time you've fought harder than me.
Thank you for not letting me destroy you, no matter how much I wanted to.
Thank you for growing and for forgiving me.
Thank you for reminding me where I've been, and just how far I've come.

Thank you for showing me that no one, not even I have the right to hurt me.

Thank you for allowing me to be creative with you, to permanently change your appearance through ink. At least we have some artwork on our walls now.

Dear body. You are not a walking apology for the things that have happened to you. Look at you, you've been curled up in hiding from the world. What are you doing? You're a lion. You're fierce and strong. Shake out your mane and practice that roar and show the world that you're a force to fight for.

You are more than a trigger warning, sensitive content that some may find offensive or disturbing. You are a statement; you show the world that you can make it. That fate doesn't make you scared, and that there's a future out there.

Hair.
I've cut you, straightened you, bleached you and dyed you
More times I care to remember.
You've been a constant rainbow for so long.
But you're still holding on
And you let me hide behind you
When I'm feeling unsafe.
Because like me, you too are strong.

Stretch marks.
I am sorry that society has taught me to dislike you.
I am sorry for all the times I called you fat - which you weren't. But even if you were, you're so much more than that.
Thank you for reminding me I've allowed myself to grow.
The bones I once could see, I can no longer feel.
And I'm sorry for the constant measurements.
My xylophone ribcage and painful hipbones are no longer here, and that's okay for me to say.
I no longer need the tape measures and notebooks of weights, and I certainly never needed the hate I showed towards you.

Dear body
Thank you for reminding me, I have nourishment and that I deserve to eat.

Feet.
Thank you for allowing me to move. To walk around the world.
To dance. You keep me grounded when I need to be but you still allow me to fly and to jump for things just outside my reach. You allow me to run away from danger, and you too, show me how far I've come, and all the new places I'm get to find.

Mind.
We haven't always been the greatest of friends. I am sorry for

treating you like my worst enemy, when you're actually the oldest friend I'll ever have. But even still, you protect me and you still think I'm worth that protection. I do wish you'd ease off sometimes, you're a little bit oversensitive, but you've meant I've never been alone. You allow me to create. You allow me to write and to perform and to communicate.

Thank you for being you. Thank you for not letting society judge us when our scars are on show, when we panic, when we walk through city centres dressed as a skeleton, for an event in April. Thank you for always, always being true to yourself.

Dear body. I owe you so much more than an apology. I owe you more than a thank you. I owe you a thank you for surviving. A thank you for everything. A thank you for loving me when I most certainly didn't love you back.

From today

I promise to love you, to cherish you, to comfort you.
To be honest with you.

In sickness and in health.
To be kind. To be patient, and to be forgiving.
In happiness, sadness, and in everything in between.
I promise to remind you that you're so much more than good enough.
I promise to try to be your friend, if you'll let me. I promise to make sure you eat, to wipe your tears and to remind you - daily - that you are beautiful.

Dear mind, dear soul, dear body.

Happy Birthday.

About the Author

Bethany Rose is an old fashioned romantic, but between her typewritten lost letters and hand dried flowers, this punk princess is a fiercely passionate spoken word artist. Sharing stories of love, loss, and internal mental battles with herself and the world around her, she will show you a world deeper than your darkest thoughts. Be prepared to see the overspilling mind of a young woman who's seen her world crumble into heart shattering pieces through no fault of her own, attempting to rebuild herself into something more beautiful.

Bloody Mary
Moya Clark, age 24

I can't remember exactly when it started, long enough ago that it has become a habit and when I was young enough not to know how dangerous it could become. I do remember, though, that it wasn't the nightly custom it is now. At first it was just a few fleeting thoughts, quickly manifesting into actions that grew into sequences, into the reluctant ritual I find myself returning to.

It is no longer a question of whether I want to find myself standing alone in my bathroom each night, but that I need to.

The ritual starts innocuously enough with the sun long set, the clock hanging on the wall provided with only enough light to tell me that it is midnight. Some call it the witching hour, but that's traditionally 3AM. I suppose 3AM doesn't hold the same poetic resonance as midnight. Either way, this inaccuracy does not stop the aberration appearing in the mirror before me, as if emboldened by the anonymity the darkness provides.

Bloody Mary. Bloody Mary. Bloody Mary.

Say her name three times and she will appear; every kid has heard the myth. Not many remember it as an adult, nor do they actually see the phantom they're trying to produce.

With the frequency I see this image, it should no longer shock me, yet each time I draw a sharp breath. Perhaps it is just part of the ritual now, just like the unwavering stare that searches each and every gruesome detail as though I had not memorised every detail in the endlessly stretching days before tonight.

The overall composition is bloated like a decaying corpse floating along the river, listless and full of waste from their surroundings. Individual details are no less disturbing, with smears of deep purple below each eye that sink back into the socket to rove around with a deep-seated anxiety. I cannot tell if this anxiety arises from their appearance or perhaps the appearance is the result of their anxieties and sins manifested. Hair strains to the floor and flies at angles away from the scalp, elongated and wisping as if it is repulsed by the body it has been forcibly attached to. The skin is stretched taut across the layers of fat beneath, thankfully hidden from the eye but attempting to break free in angry red gashes across the bare abdomen and distended hips that widen the figure to take up more space, more chance to force your notice. A decoration of discoloured patches piece together areas where they must have attempted to heal themselves from whatever it had self-inflicted in its stretched state. Whether it was unintentional is a question that lingers in my mind, as its substantial size could not make for delicate movement.

In summation, an abomination.

I let out the long breath I had been holding since the start of this silent staring contest. My eyes still level with the paranormal personage of Bloody Mary, clear before me as evidence of the mythical lore and summoning.

Yet I have been silent and the reflection staring back at me is too familiar to be an otherworldly spirit. Still, the same terror I felt as a child stood in the dark summoning the stuff of nightmares floods me. Back then there was a small part of me that knew it was all fun and games, that the light would come on and I'd laugh it off before going back to reality.

I wonder where that part of me went and when it disappeared.

Looking back on my past allows me to see the present and a hollow maw opens in my chest, just as it has done countless nights before, as I recognise each flaw and facet of the phantom as my own.

I look at myself, staring ahead and impose each terrible thought of the monster I now recognise onto my own self-image.

The despair that is written across my face is echoed back four-fold in the reflection and only exaggerates the deformity, my open mouth pushing back more folds as previously unseen fat now protrudes below the quivering chin.

It mocks me. I mock myself.

A call outside the four walls I exist within, sharp and discordant, brings me back from the mirror world before me. Back to the cool tiles below my feet and the bitter sting of the night air that has raised goosebumps along my arms. I shake as though the oppressive atmosphere could disappear with that one movement, that what I had created so easily could be exorcised just as quickly.

This reminder, of my own physical being and my own role in this nightmare, stirs a thought that calls for action.

I press my fingertips to the glass, waiting for them to pass through the surface and into that world of distortion. Confirming that I do not belong within this world but with the abominations of myth and horror that people see out of the corner of their eye, in that momentary flash where you question what you see reflected. They do not, instead I feel the tangible weight of my form press into the surface and I am grounded back to reality. Thoughts of ghosts and ghouls chased off by empirical evidence, the mental sense of here and now in the physical sense of my touch to the glass.

A sigh and click bring light to the enclosed space, making it wider and the blinding flash dispels the dark facsimile to be replaced by my true reflection.

In the light, I can see my authentic figure.

I am nourished, evidence of care through providing for myself, rather than fattened as a pig to the slaughter.

My eyes glint with mirth as realisation dawns, drowning out the rings around them - though they themselves are proof that I cannot be slowed down and will grasp every waking moment to experience that I can.

My hair flows down my shoulders, a frame to my face, unrestrained and untamed as I can be when passionate and lost to the moments of pure joy that can be found in life.

Each scar and blemish a story; proof of a life lived and appreciated in action.

The planes and curves that make up my being are displays of my complexity as a human, not able to be contained in a simple silhouette.

It is not picture perfect, but to be so would be another form of deception just as the previous had been.

It is the truth, and it is beautiful in a way that acknowledges all of me - not what is carefully chosen and manipulated through my own lens or that of others.

With a laugh, audible relief, I turn away from the mirror and step back out into the corridor to face reality.

About the Author

Moya is a true born and bred Northerner, having lived in North Yorkshire her entire life - aside from a brief stint in the foreign Midlands to pursue an English degree. She hopes this pursuit and her dream to publish her, and others', writing doesn't see her becoming another stereotypical, penniless creative. She posts when inspiration strikes on Twitter @moyasmessages and on a Wordpress of the same name.

Dancing to Acceptance
Sophie Rebecca, age 39

My journey to accepting my body has been long and hard, like many others. In fact I'm still on this journey; I believe I haven't that much further to go, but deep down I know this is likely to never end.

My earliest memory of becoming disillusioned with my body was when puberty started. My body started changing in ways I didn't like, getting more hairy, more muscular, more sweaty; lots of things that made it hard to love my body. You see I'm part of a minority of people (less than 2% of the population) that is transgender, more precisely I'm a trans woman (though at this early stage of my life I hadn't realised this yet) so these changes were particularly jarring to me, but I didn't fully understand why.

Into my late teens and early twenties I struggled to maintain a healthy weight. I didn't care for my body as it had let me down; I didn't have the curves of other girls, I had more hair and bigger muscles, so why should I respect my body? It was certainly very hard at this stage to love myself or my body, as it had morphed so far from what I felt it should have been. Through my twenties my weight would bounce from obese to normal. On several occasions, in an attempt to get healthy, I'd join gyms and work hard to get back into shape, but of course all this did was increase the muscle size that made me feel so terribly uncomfortable in my own skin.

When I first sought out help for my gender dysphoria (the

medical term used to describe someone who is transgender) I had quite a horrific experience. The people who were meant to help me made me feel even less comfortable in my skin; I was told that should I take the journey to correcting my body, I would end up as neither male nor female, that I'd be something different, that no one would ever love me. This was from a medical professional supposed to help me. It instead set me back many years, and I believed I was some kind of monster – after all, all that was represented in the media and movies of people like me was either derogatory or relentless mockery.

Eventually in my early 30s I could run no longer, I had to face who I was and I found out there were ways I could correct my body. I guess the easiest way to explain it is that I've always been female; testosterone changed my body so that outwardly I didn't look female and this was the root cause of my hatred for my body. I found out there was something I could do; I could correct the hormone balance in my body and it would correct itself. This process would take years but it would happen, and I could potentially finally start to feel better about my body.

At the same time I'd started dancing, ballet was something I'd always wanted to do as a child but had been prevented as I was perceived as male. I also didn't want dance to just be another place I was forced to conform to a gender I'm not. It was very hard to find a teacher who would accept me and teach me the female variations, but eventually in my early 30s I found someone who just saw a student willing to learn, and as long as I worked hard and improved, she would work with me. Ballet as an outlet for my emotions helped my mental state immensely. There was also something empowering about learning to control my body, to make it move in beautiful ways, to take back some of the control I'd lost when my body had first started to change. But there was a downside; like all physical activity, dance started to mould my body, it became a lot stronger and muscular, and anyone familiar with a dance studio knows there are mirrors everywhere. It was hard; here was this art-form I'd long loved to do that made me incredibly happy, but looking back in the mirror was still a man, a more muscular man than ever, even though clothed in a leotard, tights and a skirt, the frame displayed was not one I was comfortable with.

Luckily, within two years of starting ballet I also started the journey to correcting my body. Many people call this a transition but I've never liked the term; I'm not transitioning from somewhere to somewhere else; I'm rolling back the damage testosterone did to my body,

This is kicked off at first by blocking the production of testosterone and introducing oestrogen to the levels of any other woman. This essentially causes a second puberty (trust me, it sucks no less the second time through) and my body to change in many ways that would finally turned the tide. Just knowing that my body wasn't going to get any more masculine helped my mental state tremendously, but I had to be patient as these hormone changes take up to five years to happen. A majority will be done within a year or two, but things such as breast growth and bone mineral density changes can continue for 3-5 years.

Within the first months I'd noticed many changes. I'd lost so much strength I'd officially lost my duties as the house jar opener! My skin was much less oily as my pores changed, giving me softer smoother skin; my body odour changed from a musky metallic smell to something less pungent; my eyelashes grew thicker and longer; my body fat moved from my belly to my hips, bum and underarms as well as distributing around my face; and of course finally my breasts had started to grow. All these changes, however small, helped me see the beauty in my body: it was finally developing the way it should have all those many years ago.

I've spent over 4 years having laser hair removal to rid my body of the course black hair and the hormone changes ensure that they won't come back; this has so far been the most painful experience I've ever had. Being zapped by a laser over your whole body in 10mm increments for two hours every 6 weeks is a bit like torture, but hopefully will give you some idea of how painful seeing such a hairy body was to my mental health to endure such a process.

I've also explored facial surgery, but am very wary of the risks associated with any cosmetic surgery. Plus, I've also noticed that the areas of my face that I see as masculine are also present in many other women, so I'm acutely aware that these are social expectations of beauty and femininity that I've grown up exposed to. There is beauty in every face regardless of the social expectations.

So you're now pretty much caught up to where I am currently; I'm still on my journey, I've been lucky enough that even as an adult ballet dancer, I've had opportunities to perform nationally and internationally. I spend a huge amount of time in a dance studio on a weekly basis and travel all over taking classes and performing. Of course, the world of ballet can be especially hard on body image; I'm constantly surrounded by dancers who are much smaller, thinner, prettier and better dancers than I am, and I'd be lying if I said this didn't affect me. It's been a very hard journey to finally start to love my body, but the hormones have made it change to how it should have been, and my dancing means I'm in control of my body and the incredible applause at the end of a performance means the audience appreciate it too.

If I could go back and tell myself something, it would be to hang on; don't let society dictate to you how to feel about yourself. Expectations of what is a normal, perfect or beautiful body are rooted in antiquated beliefs that we should move on from; there is beauty in every body.

About the Author

Sophie Rebecca is a Chief Information Officer at Learning Health Solutions, where Sophie architects large scale IT systems to deliver better patient care and manages a team of engineers to deliver these services. Sophie's real passion is ballet: she has travelled internationally to perform for audiences despite being a late starter at the age of 34 and continues to embrace any opportunity to dance and to encourage others to dance.

Self-compassion: The Real Key to Loving Your Body?
Mandy Hopkins, age 25

Growing up in the noughties, I always thought magazine culture was the most damaging thing for women and body image. I remember touching on the topic at school (although never as much as it should have been). As someone who never read women's magazines, I felt I took a passive interest in the matter. Advertisements on TV affected me more, with products promising to transform me. The fact I needed to be transformed subconsciously reinforced that idea that at a base level, I must be inadequate.

Comparisons between the self and celebrities or models contributed to dangerous ideas about perfectionism. Talking to my friends and family now, the idea of perfectionism comes up again and again. Even when watching films and music videos, I'd compare myself to the women I saw – 'oh they're so thin, their hair is so perfect, their skin is so clear. I don't look like that; no wonder people think I'm ugly'.

Bullying at school didn't help the matter. Girls would regularly pick on me for my looks, leaving rude notes on my desk about my appearance. Once when I was only 12, I remember a group of older boys leering at my appearance and jokingly asking for a date – as if they would ever go out with someone as ugly as me! Everyday bullying like this in real life made the constant images of perfect women in the media even worse.

In the present day, I feel the impact of media has shifted. When I was growing up, as much as images of perfect, airbrushed celebrities and models were damaging, I still maintained a sense of 'them' and 'us'. I drew comparisons, but at the end of the day, they were still a 'celebrity'. They still existed as 'other' to the self, as their celebrity status put them in a different category to me. I could keep my distance a bit, because they weren't 'real.'

Social media has changed all this. I'm sure by now everyone has heard, is even bored by, the old 'social media is damaging' argument. But we can't avoid the fact that this is now the main place where women see body image representations. Instagram is the worst; specifically designed to revolve around photos, there's no escape. The rise of influencers means the them/us dichotomy has broken down. These women didn't become famous through films or TV. They're 'everyday' women who rose to fame online in a way any of us could if we wanted to (or so we are told).

Now the comparisons are stronger than ever before. They have become more real, as we're seeing images of 'real people's' bodies, including our family, friends and neighbours.

Of course, where social media differs to the old media experience is that everyday people also have the ability to fight back. The rise of the body positivity movement reflects this. Women (and men, but I focus on women here as this is all I have ever personally experienced) have responded to images of 'perfect', 'unattainable' bodies by posting confident, proud images of bodies of all shapes, sizes and abilities. I have a friend who says she has found her people on Instagram in the body positivity movement. She now has the confidence to post pictures of herself online that she would never have posted before – and I'm so, so happy for her.

But with me, and I guess this must be the case with others, I've found body positivity can still backfire. One of my house mates from university recently started a blog where she's opened up about having an eating disorder. I never knew when we were at university, and I still feel immensely guilty for not noticing. But through her blog, she is sharing her story, and hopes that by doing so she's helping others. I think this is amazing and incredibly brave and I hope it helps others like she wants it too.

However, on her 'about' page, she's posted a picture of herself. It shows her happy, smiling and eating cake – yet she's also in gym clothes with her flawless six-pack on display. I know what she's saying: 'look, you can eat cake and still have an amazing body too!'. But all I could think was 'wow, she looks great, better than me – how come she can look like that and eat cake?!'.

This response made me feel incredibly uncomfortable. It made me feel that even when other people's intentions are good, where they hope by posting real pictures of themselves, they'll help others see bodies like theirs and boost self-esteem, it can cause problems. Body positivity still, essentially, involves looking at copious photos of women and their bodies, and I think the human brain cannot help but draw comparisons. Self-criticism like this is made so much worse by social media.

However, I feel that there is a solution, and it's called self-compassion. Social media is there. It's not going away anytime soon. Avoiding it might seem like the best option, but this becomes more and more impossible if we want to keep up with friends and get on at work. Social media has unofficially crept into so many people's jobs – it might not be on the job description, but most of us are expected to do it.

Self-compassion is something I've begun to explore a lot recently after finally accepting that my perfectionism, rather than motivating me to make me a better person and to excel in life, is holding me back. I've realised how I talk to myself. If I find out my friends have (quite innocently) gone out without me, rather than thinking, 'I'm glad they had a good time, I know they enjoy doing that activity and they know I don't', all I think is 'They've not invited you. You should try harder to be a better friend – you're so socially awkward, no wonder no one likes you, you're not funny or interesting and must be a really boring weirdo to be around'.

This attitude translates to body image as well. If I see a candid photo of someone looking amazing in a bikini online enjoying their holiday, I think 'They look great. I never look that great. It's my fault for eating too much junk and not exercising enough. I'm lazy and complacent. I should do better'. I use self-criticism to attack myself, to try and make me improve myself.

Self-compassion has taught me this: talking to myself in such a critical way doesn't motivate me. It doesn't make me strive to be better. It drains me. It sucks the life out of me. I'm my own private bully. If I had a friend who came up to me worried about their body, I would never dream of saying something like that to them – what sort of friend would I be? I would try my very hardest to be kind, encouraging, and supportive, and to point out all the beautiful things about them. So why do I say things like that to myself? I should be positive about myself, my life and my body. Not only would I be helping myself, it would also help me to support others better!

My journey to self-compassion is far from complete. In fact, it has only just begun. But I feel it is a step in the right direction. It is the key to navigating through life. Rather than looking at pictures of others bodies and feeling inferior, it is teaching me to see and celebrate all the beautiful things about them, and as part of that, celebrate all of the beautiful things about me too. Self-compassion is important in all aspects of life, with body image being a big part of that.

About the Author

Writing, for Mandy, is a personal hobby. She is a history graduate who for years wrote constricted, factual essays. She therefore loves the freedom creative writing offers. Mandy spends a lot of time feeling like she's a square pin in a round hole. Body image, what it means to be 'female', and how she feels about the modern world often don't seem to align with what people around her are saying. Writing helps her to figure out her own thoughts, and find comfort through words – and when someone else relates to them, she doesn't feel so alone.

Whipped into Shape: Body Image in Performing Arts
Esmè Smithson, age 23

Here is something ironic; the height of my body image issues came when my body was actually at its strongest, sleekest, and slimmest. I don't mean that I finally hit that mystical goal number on the scales or could finally fix my belt on the smallest notch, but that my lifestyle at the time lent itself to being in excellent physical shape. Working in the performing arts industry I was dancing daily, hitting the gym, focused and determined to look my best, to be at my best. The paradox is that living my dream of working as a performer was also the situation that made me most aware and unhappy with my body.

Being onstage is a feeling like no other – the combination of adrenaline and the knowledge that you are capturing the attention of your audience in a world where there is so much to consume for a few precious moments is a powerful experience. There is an intense satisfaction in nailing a routine or song, of knowing what you are doing is impressive, that you were the person chosen for this particular section because you were the best and proved so at an audition. You are aware that you are physically able to do something that isn't a common skill, that you have trained and honed your potential into a force you can release at will and are choosing to share it for one moment in time that cannot be repeated.

Knowing your body can handle the rigour of three hours of sweat and stamina, be pushed to the limits of its strength and make it through should be, and is, a point of pride. Yet life as a performer, I personally found, deals out few of these moments in comparison to the overwhelming anxiety that is dealing with body image in this industry. The performing arts college where you were constantly pitted against peers you considered friends, by teachers but also your own mind that traitorously looked to the girl next to you and blanked out the hours of laughter and inside jokes to see only her trim waist and compare the added inches on yours. The endless auditions where complete strangers had the power to make your self-confidence plummet just by entering the room in a sports bra that showed off a toned stomach while you had squeezed yours into 'fat pants' to try flatten the bump left by last night's meal - (obviously, you skipped breakfast this morning to avoid further enhancing it) - despite desperately doing crunches in your bedroom. The blank faced panel, who don't care that you went to the gym every day this week and haven't touched chocolate in a month in order to look your slimmest for their viewing pleasure, might not even notice you if the timing doesn't work out in your favour, and can ruin your mood for hours by cutting you from the room without a second thought. It's an industry where first impressions are the basis of your entire career and if you can't keep up with that pressure, that's no one's problem but your own.

I spent three years at a performing arts college and two years working in the industry with this feeling gnawing away slowly at me. I don't remember the first time I looked at myself and was unhappy with what I saw. Some days seem more prominent than others – avoiding my reflection at the ballet barre so I wouldn't see any lumps and bumps through my leotard – while others the thought barely crossed my mind. But somewhere along the way it became lodged in my mind that I didn't look right, didn't look as good as the person next to me, as the person who got a recall when I didn't and I felt that nothing I did could change that.

Somewhere in my brain there is a disconnect, a missing wire between seeing what I look like and knowing what I look like that goes on the fritz every now and then. I don't know if it came from being in performing arts or if it was always there, simply exacerbated by the daily panic of thinking I didn't look right, but it lingers to this day. I've stood in my underwear in front of a mirror to take 'before' pictures prior to some health and fitness kick, only to look back at them a month later when my headspace was calmer and wonder exactly what weight I was hoping to lose. Through the lens of my phone camera I have warped my body into something it isn't, the original evidence of how desperately I needed to change actually working as the ultimate proof that I didn't. Besides, even if I had put a few pounds on and my jeans felt a little tighter, why was that a bad thing? Why was I so stressed about being the smallest size that I needed photographic evidence to urge me on when I am fully aware that people come in all shapes and sizes and look fabulous? Any time I try to dig into the paradox of why being bigger was beautiful on anyone as long as it wasn't me, I can only attribute it to society telling me that I have to be skinny to be attractive; in the performing arts world that is amplified tenfold because I also have to be skinny to be talented.

I decided this year to not go back to the performing arts industry; I had finished a six month stint in Spain (which had been a mental health trip all of its own) and came home slim from the constant walking, dancing and hot weather, not to mention a few weeks of dieting to fit into my end of season party outfit. I took Christmas off, finding a temp job I loved to fill up my days and earn some money and just enjoyed being home for a couple of months. When January rolled around, I imagined walking into an audition, with tan faded and Christmas indulgence at my waistline, and felt like crying. Then I did cry. Several times. I did a personal training course to put off making a decision, but when that was completed and the search to find a new job loomed before me, I knew I had to consider my options seriously.

Were those few precious, powerful moments onstage worth the rest of my minutes, hours, days feeling like this? After five years of varying levels of it, I decided no, it wasn't. And I honestly haven't regretted it since. Applying for university, keeping my part time retail job and looking for other careers hasn't magically cured me of toxic thoughts about my body image, but not putting myself into situations that inevitably end in feeling like shit about how I look has been several steps in the right direction. I'll probably always miss that feeling of being onstage, but I'm learning to find inklings of it in other avenues. Writing this, for example, has been mind-blowingly cathartic, and there's no end to the dance classes and drama societies I can dip my toe into if I need a hit of that performing drug. Anyone who has ever seen me in a supermarket queue, cooking a meal or blasting the radio in the car knows I never keep still and never shut up when I could be dancing or singing instead.

Body image in the performing arts continues to frustrate me to no end from the audience side of a stage; a West End show is applauded for their diversity by hiring one ensemble member over a size 12, but I can't help but stare at the cast list in my programme and think why only one? And does it even matter when the other nineteen girls surrounding her are trim and toned and still the far more visible majority of what the casting director wanted? Where is the middle ground like me – the curvy women and dad bod men who rest somewhere on the spectrum of size, neither 'big' nor 'small' but too much of one or the other to be acceptable for a uniformed production line of dancers? If someone can belt every note you ask for, drop into the splits on request and have the stamina to dance for three hours straight then surely their size is irrelevant. Yet audition guidelines lay out the dress sizes they're looking for because adapting an existing costume to fit a bigger size is more effort than keeping minds and dance studios open to everyone.

Would anyone really be upset if a bigger actress was cast as Elphaba when the fact she's painted green already asks us to suspend our disbelief? If Evita's ballgown had to be let out to a size 16, would anyone even notice when the classic 'Don't Cry For Me Argentina' was ringing beautifully through the theatre? The craziest part is that so many shows are about learning to love yourself and feel empowered in the body you were given; Hairspray is a prime example but the message gets a little muddied when your supposedly plus sized leading lady is actually a size 8 in a fat suit. With colour-blind casting becoming (quite rightly) more and more prominent, I think it's time for size-blind casting to take centre stage too.

I hate knowing one day I can wake up and look into the mirror and be flooded with panic at what I see. I hate occasionally being hyper aware of what I look like, of changing outfits several times to simply meet a friend for coffee as though I was still cycling through leotards and sports bras to see which I looked the slimmest and therefore the most desirable in for tomorrow's audition. I hate that it comes out of nowhere, after months of feeling confident regardless of what the scales say, that it swoops in on the attack despite the rational side of my brain pointing out I look no different than I did yesterday.

I hate that there are people who also deal with this without the support network, mostly unknowing, that I am lucky to have. Friends and family who are only aware of the most superficial level of my body image issues (me, talking about my feelings to somebody's face? I don't think so!), but help the deeply knotted ones unclench a little every time they call me out when I joke about my chubby cheeks or double chin; who compliment me without needing a prompt on both my good and bad days; who come to me to discuss their own size concerns so I can preach positive views to them and feel it become a little less hypocritical as it bleeds into my own attitude towards myself too.

Today I am happy with the numbers on my scales and clothing labels. I am not particularly toned due to moving home disrupting my gym and food patterns, but I know when I'm ready I can get back to the grind and find my rhythm again. I've put on a bit of padding, but I go the gym to feel strong and fit, not to drop a dress size. Tomorrow I might hunch over in the bath, pinching rolls of skin on my stomach; I might put a cute crop top on and post selfies on my Instagram. The paradox will continue I'm sure, but I do find that the balance has shifted in favour of being positive.

For every day I feel my thighs chafe and wobble 'unappealingly', there is a week where I admire how strong they are when poured into skinny jeans (also thank you to the internet for bringing the term 'thicc' into my life). I think all shapes and sizes are beautiful on other people and am slowly finding I think the same in regard to myself too. If I can do it, then it's about time that choreographers, directors, casting panels and everyone in the industry from award winning producers down to that very first teacher who taught you to point your toes, should be able to too. Then, maybe more people can have that indescribable onstage feeling without wading through the baggage of body image drama to get to it.

About the Author

Esmè Smithson is a former performer and forever theatre nerd who has just finished her first year of university studying Communications and Media. She loves vintage clothes, halloumi cheese, and the smell of books. Her favourite colour is yellow, and she's pleased to announce that she has officially kept a plant alive for over a year (a bonsai tree named Groot). She is a fundraising intern for the British Red Cross, and has decided if she can't entertain the world, she wants to save it instead. She also really wants a dog, so if you're reading this, please bug her boyfriend until he gives in and says yes.

Interlude 1: Body Positivity vs. Body Acceptance

Body positivity

Unfortunately, it can be seen as quite a radical move to not feel the need to change yourself in order to be respected by society.

Body positivity is a movement that wants to normalise that way of thinking. It rose from the desire to challenge the idea there was only one set of body and beauty standards to adhere to for society to deem you attractive. It recognises intersectionality, talking about prejudice against bodies based on race, disability and gender. It raises visibility for bodies that are the brunt of bullying and discrimination. It is more than the concept of self-love; it is a platform for marginalised people to speak about how they are treated differently and unfairly because of their bodies.

However, as it has grown in awareness and popularity, and become a hashtag, it has developed from the promotion of different people and body types, to feeling a secure love and confidence in your body. Hence, somewhat of a tagline born from this shift in focus: 'all bodies are beautiful.'

If you're body positive, you might find yourself relating to ideologies such as:

The body positivity movement has done a lot of good. Feeling positive towards all parts of your physical self and allowing that to build your overall confidence is a tempting concept. This ideology has done wonders for people, as you will read in this book, and I believe it can continue to do so.

But, if you're new to this world, there's no shame in recognising that this way of thinking can seem overwhelming. It can imply that feeling happy and confident depend on your relationship with your body.

If you're coming out of an eating disorder, struggling with medical weight issues or recovering from body related trauma, the idea of achieving happiness and value from just an improved opinion on your body can be a big ask.

Body acceptance

This is where I want to guide you towards body acceptance. You might also hear it being referred to as body neutrality. I like to think of it as liberation; a freedom from the idea that how you feel about your body equates to how you assess your self-worth. It is moving away from the all-or-nothing approach of either disliking

29

yourself or loving yourself. It is accepting your body for what it is and can do, and knowing that self-love is independent of how you feel about your appearance.

If you're working towards body acceptance, you might find yourself relating to these ideologies:

Again, a wonderful concept to remind you that unconditional love of your body does not need to be a baseline for happiness.

But which one do I choose?

You don't need to choose one. This is your reminder that just because you have come across these more positive ways of thinking doesn't mean you need to pick a new ideology to ultimately subscribe to.

Finding what works for you to help you move away from that feeling of self-hatred is a good start. Hating yourself is not the best motivator. It will encourage you to set unrealistic goals to 'fix' yourself and thrive in that feeling of failure when you inevitably don't reach them.

When in fact, recovery and self-acceptance are not straightforward processes. You're going have days where you love your body. You will probably still have days where you feel like crap and don't want to look in the mirror. But knowing this can help you accept that there have got to be a few dips and steps backwards amongst what can be an overall upward trajectory. Hating yourself along the way isn't going to make you love yourself any quicker.

Whether you let yourself be absorbed into a new way of thinking or you pick and choose the bits that help you most, if you're moving away from negative thoughts and destructive behaviours in favour of a kinder way of treating yourself, you're doing it right.

Self-love does not need to be 'perfect' or constant for you to be making progress; let it flow as it needs to.

To All the Internet Fatties I've Loved Before
Amanda Elliott, age 29

When you grow up a fat little girl in the middle of America, you're probably going to develop a few body hang-ups here and there. In primary school, you step on the scale in front of your entire class, and you're given that dreaded number on a slip of paper. Your friends all compare their numbers, but you hold yours tight against your body. It's no secret that you're the biggest. After all, your school chums first bullied you into dieting at eight years old. At home, your mum is constantly dieting. She says her fat body is wrong, but she says that you're beautiful, so which is the truth? Her body size goes up, then down, and back up again, but yours steadily increases. At church you're taught the evils of gluttony and excess. You learn to cover an eating disorder by calling it 'fasting.' Your leaders praise your slimmer figure. They don't ask how you are, physically, emotionally, spiritually. They just see you shrinking and assume it's for the best.

When I was younger, I never questioned the deification of thinness and demonization of fatness. When society said that fat people are ugly, lazy, slovenly, unhealthy, dirty, and doomed for an early grave, I assumed that it was true. Learning to love my body didn't happen overnight, but the Plus Size Wars documentary Channel 4 aired in 2015 planted the seeds of radicalisation. While the show was far from perfect, it featured several fat women (all white, more on that later) joyfully living their lives. These women were doing normal, everyday things like trying on clothes, eating, hanging out, working out, and posting selfies on Instagram. The documentary included their Insta handles, and I hit that follow button with reckless abandon, and that's when I truly started converting.

From that moment I followed any fashionable fat woman who popped up on my feed. I spent ages scrolling through hashtags like #honourmycurves, #plussizestylewatch, and #celebratemysize. I didn't know it at the time, but I was essentially giving myself exposure therapy. Sure, there were fat people around me in real life, but growing up I didn't see any plus size women in film or television shows, in advertising, in any mass media unless it was a cropped image of a headless fatty with the words 'obesity epidemic' underneath. In her book Happy Fat, comedian Sofie Hagen writes "The hatred and invisibility of fatness is taught to us before we even start having a language. And so subtly, that we do not even realise that it is happening. Part of this is simply because we do not see it often enough for it to be normal."

I'm not the only fat girl who has successfully practiced self-imposed exposure therapy. Self-love and mental health advocate Jes Baker says, "I've had success with this on a personal level; my body image perspective changed because I intentionally widened the amount of account types that I followed. The more diverse bodies I saw- the more stretch marks I saw, the more skin shades I saw, the wider range of physical abilities I saw- the more normalised every body around me (including my own) became. My appreciation of all bodies grew, and I started to see the beauty in EVERYONE." Like Jes, exposure to bodies that looked like mine helped my own self-image tremendously, but I found myself asking, now what?

Like any other marginal social group, internet fatties are not a homogenised group. I first dipped my toe into fatcademia when I discovered Dr. Cat Pausé's podcast: Friend of Marilyn. Fatcademia combined my love for reading and learning with my newfound self-love (or at least self-like) and I couldn't wait to dive in. I began seeking out every podcast, book, blog, journal article, and Twitter account I could get my chunky hands on. My fat internet circle widened, and two Twitter users in particular, @KivanBay and @yrfatfriend, have taught me so much about the politics of fatness. For example, they taught me about my privilege as a mid-sized fat (versus small fats, superfats), able bodied, cisgender white woman. They taught me that self-love is not the same as fat activism. Sure, my newfound confidence was great, but that was just the start.

I began to learn about the fat activist movement, and how it was a far more defiant version of what we now call body positivity, which unfortunately has been watered down and appropriated by big corporations. I learned that fat activism has roots in the civil rights movement, radical feminism, as well as socialism and other radical politics. See, fatphobia itself is deeply rooted in racism, which is something a fat white woman like me will never experience. Fatphobia is also heavily ableist, classist, and heterosexist. The more I read and the more I learned, the angrier I became. I began to see how much harder it is to navigate the world for people who are fatter than me, darker skinned than me, less privileged than me. Once again, my fat internet circle grew, and I began to seek out fat people who existed at those intersections, whose experiences were less privileged than my own.

What began as an attempt to increase my self-confidence ended up giving me a crash course in the politics of power. Because the thing is, I can be the most confident person in the room, but that won't protect me from the systems that do me harm. My self-esteem won't keep potential employers from discriminating against me, or enable me to buy clothes in high street stores where slimmer people can shop. My self-worth won't make medical practitioners take my concerns seriously instead of giving unsolicited weight loss surgery pamphlets, or enable elite universities to see that I'm just as viable as thinner applicants. My confidence won't make my body type normalised in mass media, or make me less stigmatised in society. Learning my inherent worth has been tremendously valuable, but in a way it's like putting a plaster on the symptom of oppression rather than fighting the systems curating and profiting off of oppression.

Improving my body image wasn't something that happened overnight, and it wasn't a gift from some higher being. It's something I've spent years working on: unlearning toxic diet culture, learning that fatphobia is a symptom of capitalism, unlearning all the stereotypes that I grew up hearing about fat people. Confidence has made me vocal. It's made me ask, "How do I live my life in a way that sticks two fingers up at those who would condemn me for these rolls on my body?" Confidence has made me bold. I posted my first lingerie photo on Instagram in 2015, and my younger self would be horrified, but I like to think she'd also be inspired. Finding my self-worth made me want to live loudly for her, to be the fat role model (or roll model) she needed growing up. If you're not there yet, I urge you to keep going. I'll be there to welcome you to the revolution, and lift you up as we break down these barriers together.

About the Author

Amanda Elliott is a writer, activist, and fat studies scholar. She is an avid user of the sparkle emoji, and spends her free time playing video games, reading girl power comics, and dogspotting. Glorifying obesity since 1989.

Fat Enough, Queer Enough
Ted Burr, age 30

When I was younger, the same old story was trotted out by my father to explain to anyone and everyone why I was a chubby kid. "All he used to eat as a baby was chocolate pudding!" followed by a chuckle, and maybe a hand on my head to ruffle my short hair on my potato-like head. It was something that always stuck with me, and it's something I would bring up when I was feeling a certain way, until one day in my teens, my father turned to me and said "You never really had puppy fat, you always just had elephant fat." I was somewhat bewildered; a rage would build inside my teen angst body and I would just hate myself for still being a tubby child.

Would I say that this is the start of me hating my body? No, that probably happened at secondary school. I was extremely fortunate to be able to go to a private school, but like all private schools it seems, it was sports mad. I had come from a little village primary school, not so sports mad, just quiet and quaint. I wasn't ready for this big school experience where not only was I a chubby pre-teen, but I was also effeminate. I was bullied out of the gate, made to feel less than all around.

Even when I excelled in sports – because you know, a chubby kid has weight behind him and that's good for rugby – I was still made to feel less than because I was effeminate. I'd hate getting showers after sports, so I'd hide at the back of the changing rooms, make sure all mud was off my face, and jump on the bus home and shower in the safety of my own house. Why? Well because kids can be mean, and automatically eyes were on the effeminate kid to see if he was looking a little too low in the showers.

I never did, I never would, because that would just bring about more torment for me, and being bullied by the prefects was enough. Soon enough, I'd hate sports too, and I'd dislike the people around me. I just became one of those geeky chubby kids, into things like Warhammer and 'Buffy The Vampire Slayer' – anything that would be an escape from life for me.

School would carry on like this for a long time. When puberty came about, I became a slimmer version of myself, towering above others at six-foot-three and things seemed to get better, but only because there was a way out. I had finally stopped being the chubby kid, and I was just the gay boy now, but that didn't matter because I was leaving for college.

This was the next big change, and for a while I loved myself. I became the head of a group of friends that listened to everything I said, and fell out with the same people I did, because I was the novelty bitchy gay that could have happily been a Plastic in a 'Mean Girls' spin off. I became the epitome of a teen gay, the one that I saw briefly on the TV, and that I made sure I emulated, because it was the only thing I knew. Not so obsessed with my body, it didn't particularly betray me, because I was new on the scene, and that meant fresh meat, no matter which way it looked.

For a while, I carried on happily, and I had fleeting boyfriends of varying seriousness. There was a love triangle which ended in pubic lice, then there was another triangle that ended on ultimate betrayal. There were closet cases and revelations galore, and it just didn't matter what any of us looked like, because we all had a lot more going on.

In my final year at college, I met a boy though. He was a year older than me, and from another town. He came to visit, we ended up in love and in a relationship and, for a while, it was good. We spent a lot of time together, any weekend we could really. It wasn't so bad. He cheated on me, I did all the leg work to get him back, and then I planned to move to his town for university.

All through this though, he had body hang ups. He was tall, very slim and at the time, dysmorphic with his body and eating. I didn't really know what that meant because I wasn't overly concerned with my body, or his. I'd tell him I loved him, and then we would make our little days together about eating. Making sure we had fun whilst doing so, because I thought I could fix him. I was that naïve and believed myself to be that good, I believed wholeheartedly that I could fix someone just by making them eat. Spoiler alert: it didn't work.

I slowly put on weight, he didn't, because he didn't keep up our days of eating when we were apart. It was always down to his "fast metabolism" which was the excuse we both would use. Eventually, I ended up at university, we broke up that first Christmas because he cheated again, and I just carried on my student life. That meant, getting drunk and grabbing a kebab on the way home at least three times a week. I was still oblivious to things though, so wrapped up in my social life I never really took note of anything. I was just that gay friend that would do anything you suggested and that negated any bad feelings about anything else because I felt good.

There were a few flings and relationships during university, nothing really lasting until my final year where, again, I met a boy from a different town and he just never left one weekend. I thought that this relationship would be it, everything was great, he would support me with everything and help me out as much as possible, and it took so long for masks to slip. By this time though, I had put on a lot of weight, and what happens when you put on a lot of weight and someone wants to hurt your feelings?

Yep, the insults started. We would argue at least once a week, if not more, and the insults were always about being fat, or inadequate, it was always about not being enough. Soon enough, that became a theme in life. All those throwaway comments about chocolate pudding and elephant fat became the foundations of what I would always feel. Not making a relationship last as always down to not being good enough, and these thoughts would fill my head.

I endured that torture in my mind for two years before finally walking away. I had a drive to make myself a better person, and I started to work out; I'd dance, lift weights, eat salads. Soon enough, I started to get smaller and more boys came back into my life. I ended up back on the gay scene, this time, a different incarnation of me, and people still loved it. I loved it too. The attention was always so intoxicating because it validated that I was good enough for something.

I worked out every day, I ate two meals a day – porridge for breakfast and soup for dinner. I'd skip lunch, I volunteered for night shifts so I could keep structure to my eating and off dropped the pounds, then the stones, and then the guilt. Then came other boys. Boys would want to be with me, and so we entered into the new dance of what could be relationships until one stuck.

Again, everything started out great, we would do a lot, and had such dreams for a house and marriage, holidays abroad that I never even dreamed of. But then I wasn't good enough again. I was too common, too stupid, too poor, too sexual, too attention-seeking. I kept on with my little exercise regime, and I'd post online about it, which would mean I'd get more guilt layers on top. I was showing too much shoulder, too much collar bone, I was alluding to being naked, how dare I show any part of my body.

It all became a little too much and arguments would start. Then I'd start to flirt with other people and eventually I committed the worst betrayal and cheated myself. I saw it as the only way out, and it was nice, because I was wanted, I was desired and it didn't matter if I was too common, or too poor, I was good enough for someone, for something again.

I started getting on with my life again – working out sometimes, just enjoying my own space, my own company, feeling half decent about myself – and with any occasion you find yourself back on the scene again, I was fresh meat. Well, maybe not as fresh as before, I was getting older now, but that didn't matter because I was more willing to try new things. But no sooner had I been single, that I found myself with yet another boyfriend.

He cared a lot less about me, and more about his own body, and how he could improve it. I'd suggest he not go to the gym and stay in bed, but that didn't work. So, I bought a bicycle and we would go out on them together. I was podgy by now, because I just wasn't as invested in maintaining my body as much – it was hard work and it didn't really do much for me. We stayed together for the best part of a year before he left me for his friend. His parting words "you're just not enough".

At this point, I lost it. I broke down on his doorstep. I drew blanks everywhere. I had to take time off work, and I had to deal with encroaching depression, because it was the final straw in my mind. I had endured the best part of a decade, being told that I was not enough for people, and I deemed myself so worthless, that I decided I was going to take my own life.

I was adamant. I was sure of it. I knew how I was going to do it. I had it all planned in my head. I was stopped by my mother frantically trying to get into my house as I walked downstairs to do the deed. What followed was months of self-loathing, and not caring. I drank every day, I'd not really put any effort in, I'd do anything that was put in front of me as an option and I felt like that was the best life I could hope for.

I was fairly lucky though. Out of the darkness came some light, and then a little more, and a little more. I managed to achieve things I never thought I would in a timeframe I never dreamed of, and it was sobering. I became so fixated on all the good, that whatever good came my way, I found a place for it in my life, in my home. I never even noticed how much I had changed over time. How much my body had grown.

Comments were made but I brushed them off as not so serious. It was just the mumblings of parents, and ramblings of aging grandparents, and it didn't really matter, it was only a little bit of weight. Over time though, even I started to listen, and this is when I started to feel like my body wasn't good enough. Was that always my problem? It couldn't have been. The doubts began to creep in though.

I started to look back at my life. Forgetting my childhood, and going to the point that I came out, and did everything I thought a gay man should do. I'd buy Attitude magazine and dream of living a life that I saw in those pages, that never really reflected me. People always say it's the magazines, but when you're left with just a handful that represent the person you are, and they are filled with muscle clad men, because "sex sells", you start to wonder if you were ever good enough. I held deep resentment for one man that sat as editor of that magazine. I had never met him, but he never represented me until my late twenties when body image in men began to be talked about more and they'd trot out some bulkier guy to dissect his diet and tell him how he could be better if he lost some weight, did this work out every morning before work and eat this exacting meal plan. I was already too old for that.

When, as a late-twenties queer boy, I decided to start reading more on topics of queerness, masculinity and gender, I still found deep resentment for the book the editor wrote. Why? Because it glazed over their part in queer men's body image issues, and blamed everything else, from fathers to toxic masculinity, to drugs, alcohol, clubbing, deaths. It was empty, it was void of its own realisation, and it brought no closure. This magazine had shaped me, had given me worries, and inadequacies, and it was still profiting off me.

To turn around to people and say that it wasn't until my late twenties until I really had body image issues, seems weird. People deal with this stuff for a long time, but for me, it has only felt like a short time. Yeah, I have painted this picture that stems from childhood, but it was empty words I never really listened to, because there was always something to balance it out. It took me until I was at my weakest point mentally, to ever process these things as body image issues.

It wasn't until I was thirty that I really started to own it though. That's the crazy part. I lived the life that I did, and it took me until maybe twenty-eight years old to have body image issues, and thirty years old to really tackle them face on. I began to realise that even though my body was the way it was now, that I still had the love of someone in my life, and that person hasn't left yet. I mean, I sure hope he doesn't leave because we have a wedding to attend and suits to "fit into".

This is one sticking point that trips me up even now, the conversations about our wedding and if we will fit into our dream suits in the state that we are in now. It's a trigger for me to look in the mirror and evaluate if I'm going to look good on the one day that I hope that I do, and then I have to talk myself around to being a true representation of myself. I will be whatever size I will be, and I will wear whichever suit fits at this point, because I still haven't found the motivation to stop ordering mixed kebabs at least once a month.

Do I think that, this love helped me love myself? Maybe, but it's not all down to that. It comes down to one thing – I own it. I let my body get into the state it is, and I could get it out of it again if I wanted to. I just own that even as a fat man, I can make it work. I found my place after I was approached by a production company for a television show and they called me an "influencer" and whilst people have issues with that word, it still holds power.

That shifted the perception of my body from being negative to something positive. If I could show the world my body was valid, as a fat body, in the gay community, then I could change someone else's life. That's the stance I took, and it's been my unofficial work ever since. I don't need to be going to the gym or eating salads to be valid in this space. I can forget all that and just be happy the way I am. Men don't shout "fat" out of the window of a fast-moving car at me, they shout "fag", because that's what they see first. I mean, it's not the best thing to shout still, but I take the world on as a fat, fabulous queer every day. I post online as that person, every day. I live that life, every day. Because life is too short to deny yourself the things you love, or to waste a minute on hating yourself because someone tells you you're not enough. You are more than enough and you can own it.

Not everyone is going to be told they are an influencer, but in this age of social media, anyone can make that a reality. Every word, image or video we put out into the world, influences somebody to do something. Owning that, is what changes the world. Owning it and doing something for good – that changes the world. It isn't all plain sailing.

Allow yourself to feel, allow yourself to fall, but know how to pick yourself back up again. I know that I fall probably once every six weeks, but I know that I can get back up again, because I've been further down than that before.

You can never deny your past, it happened, there is nothing you can do to change that, and I learned that long ago. But you can affect your future by living in the present, and understanding that you were always enough.

About the Author

Ted Burr is a queer advocate, body positivity activist, and podcaster born and bred in Yorkshire. He has previously written a blog for the last 10 years on what it is like to be queer, male and dealing with body image in the modern age, within the queer community before moving to podcasting on the same topics and more. Now, he produces inclusive and accessible events for the local queer community in Yorkshire, giving safe spaces for people to express themselves without worries and fears on being judged for simply being yourself.

Hiding in Fat
Madelaine Taylor, age 45

I recently had a conversation with a friend about weight loss and motivation. I considered the topic for a while and decided it might be something to share. So here is my view on weight and my own body image.

I've been overweight as far back as I can remember; I've never been bothered about my hair or my facial hair, never worried about my skin or the clothes I wear. My appearance was what it was and I never took more than a minute to think about it. Why? I was never happy with myself, with my body, my appearance or the life I was leading and I never knew why. Not consciously anyway.

Now I'm in my mid 40s and over the last four years I have figured it out. You see, I'm transgender and now I know it. Being transgender has changed many things in my life and one of them is the way I see my body.

When I first realised what was always there in the back of my mind, I looked down at my body and thought "Actually this is okay..." "I don't want to change this..." There were good reasons for this. When I looked down, I saw cleavage, I didn't see the penis that I never wanted to see. When I looked in the shaving mirror, I didn't see my Adams apple and my man's faced was softened by chubbiness. If I shaved really close and squinted and didn't look lower than my chest I could almost look like a woman! That was great, why would I want to change any of that? So, I didn't try. If anything, I was happier as I was getting bigger, and I did get bigger, going up to 140 some kilos. I was self-employed and had a car, there was very little activity in life but I was happy because I had a bra that I filled out naturally.

When I came out to my friends and family and I could wear what I wanted at home without having to worry about people turning up at my door and catching me in a dress, I became a lot happier and spent more time as I wanted. I ordered a nice bra online, and was thrilled when it came as it pushed up what I had naturally and made me feel great. My fat was very much working for me. People I knew from school told me I hadn't aged; this was down to having a chubby face that showed no wrinkles or aging lines. Having a bigger bum and thighs as well as my bust meant that I could fit in with cisgender women of a similar size without standing out too much. It also meant that the clothes I was buying didn't look odd due to my chubby curves, more or less matching their normal cut. Overall, I saw being overweight as a bonus to the life I wanted to live.

Then in May, something happened. I accepted an invitation from a very dear friend and went to Paris. When I packed, I packed trousers and tops I bought from Asda's women's department. I wore a sports bra and I styled my hair differently. I had been shaving everyday anyway at that time so that was no longer a concern. I didn't look feminine; I couldn't have passed, but I could have been seen as non-binary and that was a huge step up. I was very happy in Paris going out in femme clothing even if the rest of me didn't quite match up. I knew when I came home it would be different. I'd go back to only wearing them at home. That made me very sad.

Then I came home and I just couldn't go back to the way it had been. So, slowly I started to move toward presenting en-femme full time. By July I was walking into the town centre in a skirt, wearing (very badly done) make-up and a bra that pushed up everything I had. I stopped slyly looking at clothes in the charity shop and hovering until there was no one about so I could rush them to the till and buy whatever I thought might fit. Now I was stopping, looking and buying clothes I liked. I started shopping at Yours and openly buying make-up.

That's when I realised I had to lose weight. I knew that being overweight would affect my chances of surgery; I was worried it might affect my bloods and stop me from getting hormones but I knew all of this before. I looked at myself and looked at clothes and thought "I want to wear that, I want to look good in this."

Losing weight will bring problems that I will have to deal with. I'll lose my cleavage, I'll be able to see my Adams Apple and worst of all... I'll be able to see my penis. That's something I don't want. But I can deal with these things. I can pad a bra and make a gaff and I can use make-up to reduce the Adam's Apple issue. On the other hand I'll be healthier, able to have surgery and not worry so much about my bloods. And I'll be able to buy that LBD I really, really, want and actually wear it!

It's important to me to lose weight. Not because being overweight made me sad, not because I feel that I don't fit in or that I feel any pressure to be thin from society or media. I don't want to lose weight to make life easier for me, because honestly, losing what the fat gives me will be challenging. I'm doing it because I want to ensure that I'm in the right state to receive the treatment I want when the opportunity finally arrives. I'm doing it because going down a size or two will make buying clothes easier and cheaper. I'm doing it so that when I'm shaving my legs or painting my toes, I don't have to manoeuvre my belly first to be able to reach.

If I'm entirely honest, the truth is that if I had the money, I'd opt not to lose too much of the fat but to move it. Moving fat from my stomach to my hips and breasts would be ideal, keeping my curves and losing a bit of my belly. There are places that can do that for the right price. Unfortunately, that isn't within my reach and wouldn't help with the surgery situation. So, losing weight is currently the best thing for me.

I started monitoring my weight and calorie intake at the beginning of August and my weight is going down. I'm not doing a modern diet: no weekly meetings or special diet bars or shakes for me. I'm simply noting the calories I eat and getting a good balance between what I take in and what I use. Ironically, I'm eating more than before but fewer cheap sweets. Quality over quantity in terms of dessert has been my watchword and having regular intake, instead of eating nothing during the day and binging at night. Week by week I'm getting closer to my goal. Of course, my boobs are going first and that's annoying, my bra doesn't fit anymore and my belly feels just as big. My shoe size is going down which is a bonus and something you might not expect. In the end I'm motivated because I really want the surgery and I really want that dress!

About the Author

Madelaine Taylor is a writer and blogger from Northumberland. Living on the North Eastern coast, battered by its freezing winds and rains, she spends as much time as possible in her cosy apartment writing. You'll often find this 45-year-old Northumbrian sat with a large mug of tea, wrapped in a blanket staring at her iPad and tapping away on a keyboard. Inspired by the works of Pratchett, Eddings and Tolkien, as well as the beauty of her home county, her work often contains fantastical elements and humour. Madelaine's blog, "Being Maddie", is inspired by her journey through self-discovery. Sometimes serious, sometimes humorous, always heartfelt and genuine.

Beauty, Body Confidence and Bravery: The Story of Positively Me

Jessica Shire, age 22

Growing up, I always remember being different to other people. As a child, I wore a feeding tube up my nose because I'm incredibly underweight. I have always had a wonky chin and teeth too. Although there was nothing medically wrong with me, throughout my childhood I spent a lot of time having investigations and attending hospital appointments to try to gauge why I couldn't gain weight.

Hospital appointments and the tube feeding were normal to me but to other kids in the class, they weren't. Sadly, this meant that a lot of my childhood was filled with bullying.

Because I was different to others, I was called 'ugly' or made to feel like something was wrong with me. Throughout my time at primary and secondary school, I felt as though I needed to change how I looked or wear certain clothes in order to fit in with the people around me. In high school when I saw a spot on my face, I had to cover it up, because even though this was completely normal for a teenager, it didn't feel normal to me. The bullying and name calling destroyed my confidence and left me too scared to go out without a layer of concealer on my face as I was so worried at what other people may think of me. I avoided certain clothes in case people saw how skinny I was or in case people thought that I was too childish. I had to conform to how others were dressing, to the makeup they wore and the hairstyles they had because being different made me stand out. And that, I believed at the time, wasn't a good thing.

But a few years ago, this changed, and this was mostly down to the experiences I have had through Girlguiding. Outside of work, I help to run a Brownie unit. I also take part in many international guide and scout camps alongside this, where I apply as an adult leader to run the activities for the young people attending. Back in 2015, I had the opportunity to attend two different events which forced me to confront my body insecurities. The first place I visited was Japan for the World Scout Jamboree. This was the first trip abroad I had experienced without my parents and I was 18 at the time. The trip shaped me in my body confidence journey for two reasons. I was camping for about three weeks and the temperature out there was insanely hot. I started off in japan, wearing concealer everyday as I would in the UK to cover up my blemishes. But it became so hot, and I was sweating so much that a few days in, it just got too difficult to keep wearing it. The humidity played havoc with my hair and I was sunburned for most of the time. Because we were on a big site, the toilets and showers were basic and unless you brought your own handheld mirror, there were not many about. At the beginning of the camp, this worried me. However over time, the less I saw a mirror, the more confident I became. People from all over the world attended the event and were all having the same experiences as me. I soon realised that the people I met, didn't care what I looked like, they just wanted to get to know me as a person. During my time in Japan after the camp had finished, I went to a spa. But there was a catch - in these spas, we had to go in completely naked. This terrified me. I have never been confident enough to wear a bikini, yet now I had an option of going into a pool with other women who I had never met, completely in the buff. I said to myself to start with I can't do this, and I completely broke down. But then I thought to myself; I can't let my lack of confidence stop me from doing something that I may never do again. So, I just went for it and went into the spa. Although it was so terrifying, I'm glad I did it.

I then got back from Japan and saw an opportunity to go to London with Girlguiding to speak about my experiences with body confidence with the Dove Self-Esteem Project. I saw this opportunity and I thought after the journey that I've had in Japan, I'm going to apply for this. And to my absolute surprise (and still to this day probably one of my proudest moments ever) I got in! It was an incredible weekend and life changing. I stayed in a hotel provided by DOVE UK and I met about 15 young women from across the globe and 15 young women from across the UK to talk about an issue I was now passionate about: body confidence. We had talks from many famous people, walked down the red carpet and attended the Women in the World conference. It was just incredible. And what I learnt from this conference was that, the way I had felt, all those feelings, those moments of self-doubt… It wasn't just me that had them, other people had their own insecurities too. This weekend changed me and my perspective. After years of criticising myself, hating my body and feeling insecure, I decided that enough was enough. I realised that I didn't need to wait for validation from other people around me and I realised that the nasty comments people said about me in the past were simply not true. Nothing ever was or ever will be wrong with me.

I realised after these events it wasn't me that needed to change: it was society's perception of what beauty is and what it could be that did.

A few months after this, I saw an opportunity to film a video with BBC Three about my experiences with body confidence. I applied and got invited to go to London where I was asked to say all the comments that I would normally say to myself, to a complete stranger.

'You look disgusting', 'your skin is too dark' and 'no one will ever like you' were just some of the heart-breaking examples. This experience was overwhelming. I broke down during the video on many occasions because I just couldn't believe the extent of the nasty comments people would say about themselves. It was one of the hardest things I have ever done in my life, but by doing it, it made me realise just how harsh I was being to myself. And by discussing the comments said with another person, I realised the things I hated about my body, people didn't actually notice or even care about.

After all these incredible events, it was time to go back to my normal life and I went back to running my Brownie unit as usual. I decided after the adventures that I had had, I would talk to my Brownies (who are between the ages of 7-10) about my experiences with body confidence because the media is something that young people are now becoming more aware of and is becoming more prominent in their lives. To my surprise, at the end of the session, one of the youngest brownies came up to me and said, 'Little Owl, I can't think of anything that I like about my body'. And honestly? I felt like crying. After these events that taught me to be comfortable in my own skin, this was heart-breaking. It was awful that someone at the age of only 7 could already have these negative views of themselves. Someone so young, someone who shouldn't have a worry in the world. These were grown up problems, but yet these grown up problems were now coming after a new victim.

I knew, in this exact moment, that something needed to change. I knew then that it was important to keep talking about this issue, keep promoting body confidence to those around me and make sure that people I knew didn't feel the same way as I did growing up.

A few months passed and another opportunity with Girlguiding presented itself.

Last year, I got selected by Girlguiding Anglia to participate in their 'Action for Change Project'. This involves Girlguiding members between the ages of 14-25 going on a residential weekend to meet other people in their region and working on and carrying out their own 9-month social action project in their local community. I saw this as my chance. I knew that this was my opportunity to use my voice for taking on a project that promoted the body positivity movement. I wanted to do something brave. Something bold. Something to highlight the need for acceptance of a variety of different body types in the media. I needed to use this platform that I had now been given to make a positive change.

As a lot of the body insecurities that we have stem from social media, I decided to create a body positive Facebook and Instagram page called 'Positively me!' to promote my body confidence journey and share other people's body confidence journeys in the hope that it would make people feel more confident in their own skin. I decided on this name, because I wanted people to feel confident in who they were, feel like they didn't need to change and to have a positive attitude when it came to think about their bodies. I also decided to put on a fashion show...... with a difference: Body confidence.

Why does Body Confidence matter so much?

My Brownie was not alone in the way she was thinking. 75% of women in the UK are unhappy with their body and because body confidence can affect any gender, 45% of men do not like what they see in the mirror either. Globally, more than two-thirds of women and girls say increasing pressures from advertising and media to reach an unrealistic standard of beauty is the key force in driving their appearance anxiety. These statistics are frankly shocking and have got to change - for good. Representation matters. It's as simple as that, when someone sees someone who looks like them in the media or advertising or in the world around them, they start to believe in themselves and it gives them the confidence to go on and do amazing things. I have always had body insecurities and for many years, I believed that it was only me who thought this way about my body. However, over the years just by speaking to my friends, other people and my Brownies, I can see how much of a huge issue body dissatisfaction actually is, and the equally huge scale on which it affects people.

I believe that the issue is partly down to the rise in social media as well as the images that we see within advertising. Social media is an amazing tool, yet, nowadays, there is so much pressure to look a certain way in order to take a perfect selfie. We take photo after photo of ourselves because we are never happy with what is staring back at us. We hide behind endless filters that change what we look like and hide our so-called flaws because we feel like we need to match up with the images that we see in the magazines around us. It doesn't help that the models we see in the media always look a certain way, are a very select body shape and type, all seem to have never ending legs and there is just no variety in what we see. Let's face it, they all look pretty perfect. However, here is the truth. The models have spent hours having the clothes that they are wearing altered, or the clothes they wear are pinned up and they have had a big team of hair and make-up artists spending hours creating their certain look. The photos that are taken are then, even after all this work, heavily filtered to make the models have clear skin, no blemishes, bigger eyelashes, smaller thighs and so much more. This leads to the models themselves not even looking like the image that they see in front of them. Personally, I disagree with photoshop and think that it is over-used within the UK. When we see a photoshopped image we compare ourselves to what we see, even though the images are impossible to achieve.

Social media is great, but it craves validation. If someone doesn't get a like, they feel bad. If they don't get as many likes as someone else, they still feel bad. But this simply shouldn't be the case. It doesn't matter how people view you, it's how you view yourself which is what matters.

Not just for girls

Unfortunately, poor self-esteem and unhappiness in what you look like can affect all genders. Although it's typically perceived as just a woman's issue, this is not the case. When I go to the gym, it often strikes me how many guys are now talking about what they look like. I hear guys wanting to be bigger, ripped and more toned. There is nothing wrong with wanting to work out or go to the gym but going to the gym shouldn't mean that you have an unhealthy relationship with your body because of it.

So why did I decide to put on a Body Confidence fashion show?

It upsets me that in 2020, people like me still are not represented in advertising. It upsets me, when my beautiful friends put down clothing because they think they can't wear it because of their body size or shape, and it upsets me when my Brownies tell me that they can't think of one thing they like about their body. I've always told myself that I can't wear a bikini because people will see how thin I am, I can't wear this or that because it doesn't sit right. And this is ludicrous: fashion is made for anybody to wear and just because we see a certain type of model on TV wearing it, does not mean that it is only for that body type. The truth is that ANYONE can wear it.

It doesn't help that the mannequins that we see are unrealistic. For the women, they have long necks, graceful arms and they are drastically thin. For the men, they have broad shoulders, are tall and have an almost bodybuilder physique. The same, unfortunately, applies to some of the dolls we see in shops. A lot of brands are only showing a very specific body type and shape, when most of the population do not look that way. What we don't see is the clothes on the mannequins are often pinned up round the back and the mirrors when we go into a shop are tilted so that the clothes look differently on us. It's about representing everyone, not just a select group of people. I mean, the average size of a woman in the UK is size 12, so I believe the media has a responsibility to showcase this. I believe that no matter who you are, we all can and should be represented in the media. And if the media wasn't going to change anything, I knew that I needed to step up and do it myself. I decided to get a group of friends, family and total strangers to come together and join me for one evening to strut their stuff down my first ever body positive catwalk.

I wanted to make sure that I represented everyone, from people to physical disabilities, to a plus sized model, to someone with a scar, to someone with medical equipment, people of different ages and genders, literally anyone and everyone was welcome. Normal, real people. Incredible people who had their own incredible stories to share. I got the models to all wear something that they would never normally feel confident enough to wear and for me this was a jumpsuit. I wanted to show my friends and my family and complete strangers that they didn't need to change the way that they looked. They were unique, talented and beautiful in their own way. Running a fashion show was probably the most nerve-wracking thing I have ever done. I have no experience of event planning, or the world of fashion or fashion shows or knowing what to expect. But deep down I truly believed in my message and knew that even though it was scary, it was something I needed to do.

Quite honestly, the show was amazing and a huge success. It was probably one of the best nights of my life so far. I feel so humbled and proud of all of the brave models who came on the evening. We had talks from a charity, the models themselves, a local artist and Dove UK and even the town mayor popped along! The atmosphere was incredible and I loved every second. I can't wait until I do it again. Seeing the models have confidence in themselves, to me, was the most amazing feeling in the world. The show had that much of a reaction it even got picked up on by the local media. I've taken part in countless radio interviews, been featured in the local press and on the night had a video created highlighting the stories of the models taking part. I even got the opportunity to have an article published about me on the national BBC News website and was interviewed on both the 6pm and 10pm regional news!

Since this event, I've been hooked on the body positivity bug. I have been invited to do talks at different schools to talk about the project and its aims for the future and have published regular articles about the work that I am doing. I've even been lucky enough to have the opportunity to spread my message further to a now global audience. Before the show, I did a lot of research on body positive fashion shows and saw one that was based in America called the Dreamwalk Fashion Show.

The opportunity was to be a model in their body inclusive fashion show happening in New York City. So, I thought, you know what, if I can pull off an event in the UK, I'll give this a try too. And to my surprise- I got in! It turns out that I was the only model from the UK and the furthest travelled model that attended. I had a wonderful time at this show. It was amazing to speak with so many new people about my project and to listen to all their own inspirational body confidence stories too. Walking down the runway was exhilarating and I loved every second. It was crazy that little old me, can now say that I took part in an international fashion show! The thing I learnt about this event was that there are so many people who have body insecurities and felt the same way that I did growing up. These people were like me in the sense that we were all using the experiences that we had had in order to make a positive change.

After all of these incredible opportunities, I don't want to stand here and just be some girl with a random story whose life is now perfect because of an event I did. The truth is, it isn't, and it probably never will be. I'm still as scared as when I first started on this journey. Body confidence and believing in yourself is hard work. There are days when I still look in the mirror and find it hard to like what I see, but that's okay. It takes time and effort to love yourself, but it is so important that you do. Other people are awesome, but it doesn't mean that you aren't equally awesome too. Through my campaign, I've been inspired by so many people and gained so much confidence in my own abilities. I have really pushed myself to wear clothes I wouldn't normally wear and be a little more comfortable in what I see in the mirror. I've had make-up free days and started taking care of my skin and my body, giving it time to rest and allowing myself to take breaks. Now that I've started this campaign and have seen the impact this has had, there is no stopping me. I'm going to continue this journey for however long it takes to get normal representation in the media. I'm going to continue until each and every person likes what they see in the mirror.

And my last words of advice? I know it sounds cheesy, but don't compare yourself to other people; if you are feeling low, I promise you it gets better. You are an awesome human being regardless of what you look like and the world is lucky to have you in it. Take pride in who you are, believe in yourself and most importantly be yourself. Being unique and being different to others makes you, you! Individuality should be celebrated, valued and respected because it brings different perspectives and different ways of thinking to life. Don't change for anyone because you are enough. You always have been and you always will be, regardless of what anyone says.

About the Author

Jess is a body positive ambassador currently residing in sunny England. Through Girlguiding, she has been able to promote the message of body positivity and self-love through her Facebook page: positively me. Jess believes that normal, real, beautiful people can and should be represented in the media and she hopes you enjoy reading her piece. She wants everyone to be comfortable in their own skin and wants to spread what she has learned to as many people as possible. When Jess isn't guiding or spreading the self-love message, she enjoys travelling, eating as much cheese as humanly possible, singing and playing with her two adorable dogs.

Pavlov's Piercer
The Holey One, age 24

When most people think of body image and body positivity, they think of the way your body is presented and that you should be proud of your body no matter what shape or size; I also have this view. But what if you're generally happy with the way your body looks, but you're still not happy overall?

"I don't like the way my body looks, maybe I should work out. That might help, yeah I'll go for a run this evening. Just after I've finished eating this cheese" - Me, (circa 2013)

I've had the above thought at some stage (probably), however I found that while I could exercise to help with my occasional dislike for the way I looked, there was always something off. It wasn't that I wanted to drastically change parts of my anatomy (i.e. there's no dysmorphia here), I just felt something was missing.

Brains are weird. They're this mass of cells and connective tissue that controls everything we do. Sure, we can do things with our body, like move a muscle, swat away a fly, or flip the bird behind the back of that prick who didn't do any work in your group project that one time. But there's a lot of things the brain does that are subconscious; for instance, you can't directly control your heart rate; depending on certain circumstances your brain will decrease or increase it in order to keep you functioning correctly. But the brain isn't perfect: it does things that seem strange or it does something weird, like how you can walk into a room fully intending to tell your friend the really exciting thing you did today, but as soon as you walk past the threshold, POOF, you've forgotten it.

Which brings me onto something that will have certainly happened or will happen to you at some point which is known as Pavlovian Conditioning. It was first discovered by a bloke called, as the name would suggest, Ivan Pavlov, the basic premise is that (according to Wikipedia) you can pair a biological stimulus (e.g. food) with a neutral stimulus (e.g. a bell) and that can produce a response such as salivation. An example of this is Pavlov's Dog experiment, wherein whenever a dog was given food a bell was rung; naturally, the dog would salivate on being presented with food. However, it was observed that afterwards when the bell was rung, the dog would salivate on its own.

Now, quite naturally I might add, you might be wondering what on earth this has to do with body positivity. Well I have also been Pavlovian Conditioned to associate the smell of a certain brand of antiseptic with pain, and by extension I receive a huge spike of adrenaline. Not only this, but I can't get on a train to Leeds without getting nervous. The reason? Most of my trips to Leeds resulted in a very nice man stabbing a very sharp needle through some region of my anatomy. Most women have had this experience (and in recent years quite a lot of men) through getting their ears pierced. But let me tell you, getting your ears pierced when you're 13 is a completely different kettle of fish to be lying on a piercers table with a clamp on your penile frenulum awaiting quite possibly the most painful experience of your life (it wasn't by the way, thanks for asking).

I got my first piercing when I was 17. I say got, I did it myself which I don't recommend. I did it with a safety pin that I'd "sterilised" with a lighter, it hurt and to this day I've never quite been happy with the placement. It was during quite a difficult time of my life; I've always had an issue with depression and unfortunately turned to self-harm, leaving scars that I still bear. However, since that day I haven't turned to self-harm. I had found a different outlet – putting pieces of metal through my skin. "Hey," you might ask "Isn't that just self-harm with extra steps?". Well, yes, it is in a way; however it solved two problems I'd been having in my life up until that point:

1) As previously stated, I didn't self-harm again and haven't

since;

2) I'd found the source of my unhappiness with my self-image.

The vast majority of my piercings (tattoos and scarification pieces are also in this category) have come about through various hardships over the years: breakups, serious bouts of depression. Whenever I got a new piercing, it gave me something to look after, something to focus on. Almost like having a support pet, you need to keep yourself healthy and active in order to ensure that this new thing you've done to yourself looks and heals correctly.

When I was 20, I had left school and started a job in a software company. The pay wasn't great but the work was enjoyable and yet I still wasn't happy. I moved out of my parents' house into a small terraced house in Skipton, in September of 2015. I thought that by having my own space I would start to be happy again and get through the bout of depression that had resulted in me being a horrible person to live with. It helped to a certain point, but it didn't fix the problem. By this point I had taken out my home-done piercing and only had a nipple piercing (which is the most painful piercing I've ever had, I'm grateful I only have two of them), I assumed that I couldn't have any piercings on display for work. I was starting to fall into the same cycle of not being happy with the way I looked and I was starting to go to the dark place.

Which takes us to the previously mentioned penile piercing and the start of my Pavlovian Conditioning. I decided that since I couldn't have any piercings on display the obvious solution was to get one that only myself and a select few people would see (how wrong I was, to date more men have seen my genitals than women, by quite a large margin). So there I was in the waiting room, after awkwardly mentioning to the woman at the counter what I wanted doing, nervously shuffling my feet and trying to stop the tremor that had started in my hands. My name was called, I went into the room, said what I wanted doing and it was done. I walked out of that piercing room happy again: I'd staved off the thoughts of self-harm and turned it into something more pleasing that would make me happy for years to come (or until I felt I needed to get another one at least). Since starting university and being more able to freely express myself, I now have a grand total of 25 piercings, (18 of which are above the neck and 7 are below, 2 nipples, 4 genital piercings and a belly button), a multitude of tattoos and one piece of scarification on my leg.

It's a strange feeling, being more comfortable in your own skin after you've changed it to be different colours or to have more holes than Swiss cheese. It's also strange to be completely at ease by the resulting effect on the general public. By that I mean prior to the piercings and tattoos I didn't have any problems with interviews or getting on buses, old women didn't clutch their handbags closer to their chests when I walked by, I didn't get stared at in the streets walking around town. But when I get stared at, I don't mind; my modifications (piercings specifically), represent what I look like on the inside, they're my war paint. Yes, I've been through some shit, but I've gotten through it, fuck you, you don't know me. It's amusing the way people look and judge and for every person the judgement is different, you can see it on their faces. I find the older generation tend to be more assuming that you're some sort of criminal, because no right-minded person would do that to themselves. Some look on with admiration and appreciation, which I tend to find either with people who want to look the same or already look the same, when you are heavily pierced and tattooed and, as I do, wear your scars for the entire world to see you join this collective of people who have done the same thing. It's a support group almost. Does this mean that everyone who has lots of piercings and tattoos do it because they turned it into a more proactive form of self-harm as I did? No of course not, most people do it because they want to look a certain way, or attract similar minded people and like the way that tattoos and piercings look. But for the subset of us who do it because it's cathartic or therapeutic we're still valid in our reasons, it's not a form of self-mutilation or for the attention, it's for us, it's therapy, it makes us happy.

Nowadays my piercings aren't only a representation of a time when I was down or depressed, I get them when I was happy too. When I look at myself, I don't always see the piercings themselves I remember the memories. What kind of day it was, who I was with, how I was feeling at the time. They're a sum total of the experiences I've been through, good or bad. Some piercings are painful to think about, but then I see how happy that piercing has made me and it helps deal with it. Sometimes it's good to remember the bad times, they can show how far you've come since then, how much stronger you are from that particular time. Everyone deals with these in various ways, my method might be unorthodox but the piercings are there as a reminder that no matter how bad things get, it will pass. Time is a great healer and I find that by the time the piercing I have chosen to represent that period of time in my life has healed, I will also have healed. Maybe I haven't healed completely, but that piercing represents how far I've come since that time.

Am I saying that everyone needs to use piercings as an outlet to deal with their issues? No, I'm just saying that we need to be proud of what we've done, be proud of those parts of your body that you don't like, be proud of who you are as a person, be proud of that person who got through it and will continue to get through it and most importantly: fuck anyone who thinks anything different.

About the Author

The Holey One is a software developer by day and a metal guitarist and classical pianist by... whenever the mood takes him. He also has a peculiar obsession with seeing how much metal you can implant in oneself without setting off airport scanners.

Interlude 2: The Good, the Bad, and the Guilty

Something we love to do as people is apply moral value to our actions. This can work well for the most part: it can build character, give us guidance and help us make tough decisions. However, this process does continue to churn out one continuous result: GUILT: an indicator letting us know we maybe shouldn't have done that. Or at least, we feel like we shouldn't have done that. And to get rid of that feeling, we need to repent in whatever creative way we feel necessary.

Bringing this into body image, two large aspects that we can moralise are:

1. Food
2. Exercise

Before I look at these closer, I would like to disclaim that I am not a dietician or physical trainer. Any opinions are my own from personal experience and should not be taken as nutritional or health advice. If you do feel like you are struggling with your relationship with food or exercise, please consider speaking with a professional.

Food

Let's tackle number one first. We know there is a stigma against putting on weight and being overweight. Therefore, foods that are higher in calories and, in turn, are seen as more likely to make us put on weight, are labelled as 'bad.'

This value of 'bad' is associated with the food when we eat it. In consuming it, we then apply that moral worth to ourselves.

"Oh, I was so naughty, I had a slice of chocolate cake this afternoon."

Equally, to fulfil the celebration of smaller bodies, foods lower in calories often tick a box in our brain as being 'good.'

"Just a green leaf salad for me, I'm being good."

This sort of language around food is normalising the demonization of food groups and perpetuating feelings of guilt when we eat.

Diet culture exploits those feelings and uses them to mark our progress and accomplishment in adhering to their set of food rules. Though not the case for all, a lot of diets put certain foods in the 'bad' category and banish them from our new palate to achieve a short-term goal. If we follow these rules and start to see results, we're going to associate cutting these foods with a feeling of success.

Unfortunately, we may then find ourselves in a diet trap.

This structured way of eating is not sustainable long-term, so the first time we break this habit and eat one of the forbidden foods, we have the sinking feeling of failure which can be pretty powerful. It might leave us feeling apathetic towards eating habits, causing us to give up and rebel by binge eating the foods we had been avoiding. Until we find a new diet, and the cycle starts again. Or it could go the other way, and this feeling of failure could morph into a fear of food, which could then develop into other harmful coping mechanisms like obsessive restriction.

Either way, that's a lot of mental energy spent on judging and punishing yourself for trying to nourish your body.

Allowing yourself to enjoy all food groups is not a dismissive blanket to say nutrition is not important. The nutritional value of food is still something we need to take into consideration when fuelling our bodies. However, health is more than just caloric value and a number on a scale. Finding what works for you as an individual is the bottom line. So that when you do have that piece of food that falls into the 'less nutrient dense and higher in calories' category, it doesn't make you 'bad' or a failure. There is no 'one size fits all' approach to forming eating habits. How you choose to enjoy food may not match the latest diet craze but that doesn't mean it isn't working for your body. Instead of going to pains to fit yourself into a way of eating that wasn't made specifically for you, spend that energy on listening to your body and appreciating what is best for you.

Trying to separate your food from moralisation and find your own approach to fuelling your body is not disregarding your health. It is instead the aim to remove feelings of guilt and prevent destructive behaviours that we believe help us to relieve it.

Exercise

One of these said behaviours we can abuse is exercise. Exercise is quite a personal element of your life, whether you lift in the gym, prefer home workouts, have a daily walk, do sports, or just move your body when you feel like it, it is your choice in how you get your body moving. As is the reasoning behind it. There is nothing wrong with training for performance. There's nothing wrong with training for aesthetics. There's nothing wrong with training for your physical or mental health.

But if you find yourself training as forced compensation for what you have eaten, then that might need a closer look.

To lean back into the stigma against being overweight, we know that weight loss can feel like a mandatory and ongoing goal.

If one of your exercise goals is towards weight loss, that is absolutely fine! But it should not come at the price of your health and wellbeing. It shouldn't be a penalty for that slice of chocolate cake you have just learned how to allow yourself to enjoy.

You may have heard this phrase before, but I cannot stress it enough:

"Exercise is a **celebration** *of what your body can do, not a* **punishment** *for what you ate."*

It works the other way around as well. You don't need to exercise first in order to 'earn' your food. Your body needs you to eat whether you were able to hit the gym yesterday or not. The mental gymnastics we can do to try and work out whether we have exercised 'enough' is probably more effort than the exercise itself.

If your goals mean consistent training is best for you, then do that. Having that aim can be really useful. But if you skip one day because something else in life took priority or you simply didn't feel like it – that is okay. Listening to your body is important, and taking that time to reflect is a recognition of your abilities and can ultimately get you back on track.

Food and exercise don't have to be hard and fast rules, nor is your body public property for people to morph how they want. Go and let yourself and your body be a little unruly.

Becoming 'We'
Holly Larkin, age 35

"It began before you could speak,
Your face was grey and drawn,
You wouldn't eat but you drank constantly!
You sat in front of the washing machine, I looked at you, I knew you were dying.

The doctor said I was wrong.
You wet yourself because of your age,
I was a neurotic mother,
It was my first child, it could only be expected, me being a single mum.

By the weekend you were comatose,
I ran through the hospital with you limp in my arms, I was sure you were dead.
The doctors took over from there, it was their science that saved you, their management that dictated how we lived, where we lived and who you lived with. One slip up on my part and you would be gone, bodily departed or absent into the home of a more competent mother."

This story has been told to me more times than I can remember, although I have no physical recollection of the events. It feels like my memory; I see it in my mind's eye.

It invokes distress on multiple levels: the near loss of a child, dismissal of a mother's innate knowledge that her child is dying, entrance into a new world by which medical science possesses the relationship between mother and sick child.

It is my mother's story, and it is mine.

When I was 18 months old my body became a ticking time bomb.
Daily injections to manage my inability to create insulin,
daily blood tests to monitor what that artificial insulin was actually doing to me,
night-time hypos that required a mixed cocktail of honey and apple juice,
seizures when the night-time cocktail was too late,
constant checks by white men in white coats who knew how my body worked better than me, or my mum.

And the constant threats that hung over our every move;
threats that I would die right now
threats that I would die soon
threats that I would die young
threats that even if I managed to somehow survive, there was a physical price to pay.
I would go blind,
would have my feet amputated,
my legs amputated,
all of my limbs amputated.

As a child, I was exhausted most of the time,
my body needed constant monitoring,
and it still did whatever,
it felt like.

Playing games affected my body, made me sick in one way or another.
So, I sat, and I read,
on my own.
Reading was my safe place.
We had a reading time every week, it was often interrupted for

hospital appointments.

On one occasion I was especially pissed about my reading time interruption;
I was in my final year of primary and was reading a horror story.
We got to the hospital and my doctor mentioned puberty.
He asked my mum to leave the room so that he could do a physical exam.
It went too far,
he smirked as my eyes widened in shock.

Later, my mum told me he had raised a concern to her that day, worried that I could be suffering sexual abuse.

I said nothing.

When I did speak, it was dismissed,
It was forgotten.
Professionals in positions of power don't behave like that.
But they do,
and he had.
Nothing ever happened about it.

My sick body and my sexual body became intrinsically linked.
Being unwell gave me free access to body controlling systems. Get sick enough and the weight disappears,
it felt like control.
The only bodily control I had ever experienced.
The endorphins made the pain in my body manageable, people told me I needed to accept my illness. They told me I was angry. Said I was a difficult teenager.
No one ever asked me why.

Being sick was a great defence mechanism.
There were plenty of men who wanted to provide me with things.
A home that I could serve them in,
sex to calm my irrational anger,
a baby as a reason to exist.
Men dictated how I lived.
Men dictated where I lived.

Men dictated if I lived.

They punished me when my disease did not act in the way they had designed.
They embarrassed me, told me I was a lazy and disobedient sick person.
Rational scientific evidence had no space for a resilient and angry girl.
Being sick made me too much to handle.
Marriage material means providing, not receiving, care.

So, my existence hung in the balance between keeping men at a safe distance, and just about staying alive.

But I felt like shit.

My escape was accidental. I discovered I was smart, really smart.
It gave me something to live for.

My body disagreed.

I lost my independence;
24-hour care from my family,
waking in a pool of sweat,
waking in a pool of piss,
barely waking at all.

Then a new team of doctors,
all female,
all quiet when it mattered.

They finally asked me why.

The technology I received felt intrusive, constant attachment to my body.
People would see that I was different.
My invisible disability would be available for the world to view.
It felt uncomfortable,
I felt like a freak.

Then I started to notice the same technology on other bodies.
I could see my community
I could speak with my community
I was not alone.

I began to feel proud.

Unzip my dress and you face a nest of wires,
remove my underwear to observe a layer of cannula inserts,
attempt as you will, my body can't be detached from its machines.

My body tries to control me still,
tries to throw me back into the arms of male medics.

But it fails.

I have cyborg qualities now,
disease and robotics struggle to co-exist, they both want complete
control.
This fight is mine,
I have my algorithmic soldiers,
I tell them how to behave,
I tell them how we fight back.

And I have my community.
People who know what it's like
People who live what I live
People who believe me.

Together we beat this shared body,
together we conquer this bodily space.

This space is finally becoming ours.

About the Author

For over 30 years, diabetes has shared a body with Holly. As her writing depicts, this chronic condition has not always been easy to live with. This disease has been a critical friend in many ways. It has forced her to question what matters, what she can live without. Holly has had to befriend it to appease it, to not do so always ends in chaos. Living with clinical guidance (throughout her life) has been a more complicated affair. A chronic health condition is with you every hour of every day, but clinicians change. Some are excellent, others are not so great. In her writing, Holly aims to narrate how much power is held in the hands of clinicians, and how their choices, perceptions and ethical commitments implant themselves within the lives of their patients. They can save our lives, moreover they may give meaning to what it means to live in our bodies. Healthcare is an important service for the maintenance of life however, when done well it could also save our humanity.

The Darkness Is Where the Magic Is
Coco Oya Cienna-Rey, age 49

My home life was restricted, not because there were too many rules but because there were too many unspoken ones, no clear guidelines for being. Boundaries that you set for yourself were constantly adapted because somewhere along the way they didn't fit in with how someone else wanted you to be. I came from a family background of abuse and frustration; I held back my tears and held onto my tensions. Over the years as my trapped frustration accumulated and the hurt and anger amassed, the tears would begin to fall, yet I would stop myself mid flow, unable to let go. I hung on tight from fear of feeling the hurt. There is no hiding from yourself, my body showed me in so many ways where I had hung onto my pain.

To move through trauma, one needs to get present with the whole of their being. One needs to get into the depths hidden from view to restore the suffocation of innocence. There is little room for self-acceptance when the sense of innocence is lost. My parents were not able to reflect back the essence of innocence, how could they when they never received it themselves. I have images of my childhood memories of times when I felt powerless and alone, not listened to by the adults in my life I began to learn to stop listening to myself.

This dissociation was lived through the muscular tension in my body that shut me off from feeling sensation. Withdrawing from sensation did allow me some relief but eventually resulted in numbness and the condition of chronic fatigue. Through the overriding of emotions, I lost the inner ability to distinguish pleasure and pain, I had severed body boundaries. I was a stranger to myself unsure of the burdens I was carrying and more so unaware of the burdens I wanted to put down.

The stiffness in my body, the resulting of years of secrecy, shame and silence kept a grip on my being until I choose to let go, to stop having such a strong hold of myself and to ride the wave of emotions that needed release. When I opened the floodgates I became aware of the places I had cut off from self-love. I was fearful to meet that rising energy, the pain of where I had been in contraction, the pain of where I had not fully listened to myself, my internal being asked me to rise and surrender, to give to myself the love I has steered away from. My pain was asking me to meet with my inner beloved.

I used food as a comfort and put on weight to act as protection against men's advances and to feel grounded and heavy. I stopped being nourished by life itself. I stayed in relationships that didn't work for me, I became the walking dead. I hung onto the memory of those relationships even when I had walked away. I had fear of going it alone. Not being alone, but feeling alone in the world, with nowhere to really call home. Nowhere to really rest my head when it was weary, nowhere felt safe; a legacy that came from my bed never feeling safe. He would come for me in the night. Take me into a quiet corner of the house long after everyone went to sleep. I felt his roughness pressed against my skin.

My earliest memory of sexual abuse was when I was aged two. I think it stopped for some time between then and when it started happening when I was aged nine. Piecing together the full history is still sometimes challenging. For me, domestic violence and sexual abuse was normal, particularly when there were three different family members behaving in this way towards me. The language used towards me made me very introverted and for a number of years up to my adolescence I lost my voice through fear of speaking out. I learnt very quickly to shut up and smile and to wear the fake smile of a good girl. Good girls become suppressed women. Love in the family home was distorted; it was shattered from that first inappropriate touch, a touch that told me, I was no more. A touch that told me there would be a thousand wounds to heal in years to come. A touch that made me leave my body so I wouldn't feel the searing hot prods inside your skin.

At thirteen I had a friend at school who I confided in and she confirmed my fear that his behaviour wasn't normal and that I should speak out. It took two years after that for me to tell an adult and when I was aged fifteen I told my mum. She wasn't a safe person for me to talk to, and her denial and insistence that I forget about it was a greater rejection than the abuse itself. I didn't feel safe anywhere. There was no support for me to cope with being as scared as I was, yet at fifteen I felt ready to take some of my power back from everyone concerned. I left home and struggled alone unable to communicate all that was raging inside me. Our feelings do not go unheard within the body. I experienced great periods of depression throughout my younger life and early 20s, as I suppressed any association with my abuse. I split of further form any feelings in my body. I left my body often just as I had done as a child, a way to escape the plot twist of my seemingly hopeless story.

At aged 30, I was ready to put together all the pieces of myself that had been numbed out from abuse. I wanted to create a container to hold my shattered pieces. I was ready to speak from a place that demanded the utmost respect because I respected myself and expect nothing less from others. I was ready to speak a truth that allowed me to rest and take time for myself, for I was a woman that was learning to be gentle with herself and one that had surrendered to life. I was a woman that was learning to let others hold her whilst she was learning to hold herself.

When you know it's time to change and you are ready to invest in yourself, when you are ready to do the deep work and dive into the aspects of yourself that have been blindsided because its felt just too dam hard to fight; you will go to the depths of your being and do whatever it takes to do the excavation work to reconnect to your heart. When you are ready, those aspects of the self that you have held in the dark will fight for their survival against the ones that are trying to bring you into their light. And internal war ensues; the true you against the false you that has up until now kept you safe. Those parts like abandoned scavenging children will do almost anything to stop you from doing the work. They create chaos and tell you lies that this cannot be the right thing to do. 'Look at how much conflict it's causing you,' they shout, anxiety ensures you that they must be right. So, you procrastinate and are filled with self-doubt. Life seems even more uncomfortable than it was, before you made the pact with self to grow. Small issues become big ones, an attempt to turn you away from the true path. You turn back to what is familiar even if that is trauma and pain. Everything becomes a threat. What to do when your body lies and everything you have since repressed jingles away at your bones. You learn to get still.

It's taken over forty years for me to finally come to some sort of peace in my life and begin to live my passion. Doing so however meant I had to confront every perceived fear in my being of what it meant to be a woman. Being a woman that had suffered from childhood sexual abuse I had no real interest in knowing myself as a human being let alone a sexual being, and further still I never perceived myself helping others in the world to heal from this trauma. Yet this is where I stand today.

I found creative ways to express myself, communication doesn't have to be spoken, particularly when one has experienced trauma. When you acknowledge that there is anger and rage you can learn that dealing with it is part of empowering yourself and reclaiming your autonomy. For someone who has experienced sexual abuse, the fear of talking about it isn't unfounded. There is a lot of opposition in society to acknowledging victims and how they are affected. The denial that comes from the world around you can feel as severe a punishment as the trauma itself was.

Part of the process of my healing was to establish an environment that supported me and enabled me to let down my defences, without the pressure of alertness for survival. I knew my body needed to move to free itself from restraint. Movement was discouraged in my household, often told to sit still; to be seen but not heard; to sit up straight; to watch my manners; to speak politely; to sit with my legs together, all boundaries that limiting my movement.

Movement and dance became an act of rebellion. I danced around my living room wild and free, I danced my heart out, a daily practice of movement mediation. I danced myself alive. To be spontaneous was exhilarating, to be able to let go of all responsibilities; to lose myself in the state of free flow, to allow the connection between emotions and body to unify. It was one way of being defiant against the restrictions of my body as a child; it was a way to take back some control of the space my body occupied. In those moments I transcended all that was purely physical. I was out of my body in a new way; in space and time that has no boundaries. I was learning to ride the wave to undo the beliefs that bound me. I was becoming aware of the richness of my own inner life. I was entering into an exploration of my inner world, building resilience and a willingness to wait at the edges of my knowing and step into the depths of my darkness. My body was worthy of my attention.

Before dance I felt trapped and betrayed by my body, a prisoner of its internal wars, a battled between the steadfast parts and the splintered parts that needed to be called back home. Those were the part of me that didn't know how to be, the part of me that were needy in relationships, the part of me that scarified my soul in order to be loved, that parts of me that long to feel the depth of another but would exit the body when my body was in the throngs of pleasure. Those parts saw all emotions as a threat. The journey of calling my body back has been a long one. The voices of my childhood abusers became my own mantras of internal dictatorship. My body was not my own. It became an empty vessel. I was left parched and hungry for life. I was a hungry and lawless victim consumed by her own demons. I became cunning consuming many vices; I was always up for a fight. Don't dare back me into a corner for you would have felt my venom, and I would have chew off your face just to feel safe in my own skin. Before dance I was always on high alert, constantly switched on, anxiety was my set point. The slightest thing would trigger my pain; I hated being a woman. I was the good girl gone bad carrying so much shame on my shoulders.

To embrace myself meant having to embrace all of me, to let the language of love speak though my bones. To let the language of love take over my movements. I have dance with the devil and all that was unholy, I danced far away from the shores of true love, away from the tranquillity of tender loving care; the more I danced the more I came home to myself and transmuting pain into beauty; trauma into tenderness. We are alchemical beings finding our way home. When I danced, I loved to feel the breeze upon my skin. The air became my lover, a mystical union ensued. The air an unseen hand caressing my every crevasse and curve, letting me know my sorrows were seen. When tears would fall, they would always be dried by the hand of god on the whispers of the wind. I at times was a paper doll, fragile and kept under wraps. I sometimes wished the wind would carry me away and unburden the responsibilities placed upon theses paper thin shoulders. My journey with my body changed so much over my lifespan; it can never be the same after abuse. Something is forever changed. Yet in the relationships with myself I had created the same environment internally to that of my early childhood, one in which I had been silenced or pushed away for speaking out. I wanted to break through barrier around my voice and I needed support to do so. I had to learn to listen to my wounding.

What I know is all of us are born to love and be loved; yet the road to love isn't always a smooth one. Yet it is always back to love we return. Experiencing an early life of trauma shattered me into a thousand pieces; particles of stardust waiting for the compression of pain to reform me into something new. Trauma is an alchemical process, it catalyses change and can guide you toward a path of tender transformations, if one allows. Finding the courage to be seen in all of your pain is what will finally set you free. However, one needs to feel safe in order to take risks, to come back into alignment with the heart. When we turn towards the heart, we see that our humanity is in need compassion to un-mute the secrets of the heart. Love is the hottest currency on the planet and the real purpose of generating an inner relationship with the self is to acts as an agent of change for another in the most beautiful ways possible. It can take one small gesture of compassion to build self-trust and create large amounts of change.

For years I ran away from my feminine and sexual power, I was made to feel it was dangerous and deviant. As a young girl the messages I received only fuelled this ideology more, told repeatedly to keep my legs shut as though dark forces would spew from my being if I didn't, I became even more inhibited through guilt and shaming of my body. I ran around trying so hard to strong. Infallible, forgetting my own unique feminine rhythms, I want against my true nature. Asking a woman to stay consistent is like asking the trees not to shed their leaves in winter or the flowers to push through in the spring.

A truly nurturing inner relationship has the capacity to heal from past pains, and allows you to be seen for who you truly are. True intimacy helps us see in the darkness, to shine light on our shadowy past, to reveal our blind spots, all that lies within us that we don't want to admit, see or own within. For me there was much I choose to disown and stuff down. The journey into the shadows takes courage because it shines light on all the pain we don't want to feel. The greatest gift I can give as a woman is my sound. In the world today woman have lost their voices so much that we do not know the sound of our authentic passion. I found through my healing journey that there is no part of me that I need to discard. As I learnt to trust my feminine intuition, I learnt to trust my gut. It allows an opening into the depths of their being, into the love that was always there. A love so pure that once tapped into reveals the truth that we are perfect just as they are. My silence became a choice rather than a forced condition. I began to turn inwards to find my truth and developed a practice of movement meditation. Through shutting myself off to the outside world I began to make a connection with the inner me, the real me. During my early days of meditating I began to realise the gift my earlier experiences of spitting had afforded me, as it helped me to reach levels of deeper exploration.

The deeper I went in, the more my body began to relax and let go of all the tension within yet the more I relaxed inwardly the more I began to notice outwardly aches and pains. It took physical pain for me to realise I was still in emotional pain. Through dance I began to wake from a deep sleep and I had begun to feel. The pain I had suppressed began to rise and it was felt deep within my bones. My bones held my deepest memories, the living framework of my life that flexed and changed as I did, holding all that I had been though and all that I was to become. Like the rings of a tree we bare the scares of our growth. Bones are living things, all parts of my body dependent on their hidden presence. Like the skeletons in my closet I had lock away long ago. They rattled to draw my attention to my hidden depths. My bones the storyteller of my life that would remain long after the rest of me dissolves became ridged and stiff, a symptom of the many years of secrecy, shame and silence. My body became ridged and unable to sway in the winds of change. One strong gust would break my branches and it often did. To feel safe again in your body is a wondrous gift. The power of the feminine is so subtle. My inner psyche knew what safety felt like. Sometimes it takes a little while to settle in and listen to what your body and life is telling you. It takes courage to face the feelings that arise, to honour oneself with the gift of gentleness, of stillness. To sit with the feeling that you are already whole and complete and loved and cherished just for being you. To stay long enough in the cocoon of darkness, for darkness is where the magic is. To be willing to heal those wounds of unworthiness; to wholeheartedly strip yourself bare to reveal your hidden truths; to be seen and create space in the body.

To love yourself beyond the bonds of the body to the far outreaches of your soul is truly a courageous act. There comes a time when we begin to see the symptoms as the teachers and not the enemy we thought. When we stop seeking outside the self to make things well, the body becomes the guiding compass and we learn to get still and just be with what is. And in those moments when you may stray off the path, when your fears come up and you try and tell yourself that the new thing is not a good fit. When you get really uncomfortable with where you are growing into; with your shaking knees and trembling voices know you will find bravery to feel into the butterflies of joy at the new connections you are making. When you surrender to your dark spaces and allow yourselves to listen long enough, the darkness bleeds out the truth of who we really are. Compassion is your ally; it can hold the spaces that you fear to tread.

It has been an act of kindness to see my darkness as my teacher, its pathways show where I departed away from my wholeness and discarded pieces of myself battered and bruised. It is an act of kindness to no longer say one thing with my body and another with my words; this is an act of self-love. Now is the time for the power of self-love and the power of speaking truth. And if you have felt it, even if only for a split second, that feeling of standing fully in your own power, follow that spark of light home, even if that means entering the darkness.

About the Author

Coco Oya CiennaRey is a Leeds-based creative, poet and writer. Her work has been published online and in a Rommi Smith anthology of poetry 'Check Hope Remains' and soon to be published 'narratives anthology' by Peeple Tree Press. Her writing is informed by her journey on the Tantric path and her personal experience with trauma induced pathologies. Often thought provoking, yet always heartfelt her work speaks of the sacred wisdom stored in the body, and our innate connection to the natural world. This piece 'The Darkness is where the magic is' speaks to the non-linear nature of trauma.

Reflections of a Nearly 60-Year-Old Woman
Judith Hargreaves, age 59

I exercise daily: walk, cycle, enjoy sex and swim more than half a mile a week. I eat healthily and I think I weigh around 10 stone, though I purposefully don't stand on the scales like I used to.

I am more comfortable with my body than I have been in my whole life as I approach the six-zero birthday.

It hasn't always been the case though.

Emma's project has prompted me to think about how other people have influenced my own view of my body image throughout the various stages of my life. My reflections have surprised me and revealed how much my identity, worries, and behaviour have been tied up with age, appearance, experience, self-worth, confidence and influential incidents well out of my control.

Judging eyes should never have mattered, but that is easy to say with the hindsight of years. I know what I would say to these comments and judgements on my appearance in hindsight. Thankfully my friends, politics, music and literature saved me!

Currently, my hair is grey and I cut it with clippers. I am frequently mistaken for a man as I fit the stereotype; short grey hair, trousers, biking jacket. This does not bother me at all. I am a teacher of young children and do get asked by the thoughtful, brave ones, "Are you a boy or a girl?" I know they are asking because I do not fit the female stereotype. This doesn't bother me but it does worry me. It worries me like the girl/boy pink/blue divide, gender inequality, domestic abuse (coercive and physical), raising strong girls and sensitive boys. Campaigns I fought 40 years ago along with many gender issues.

I could debate the colour pink for hours!

My son wanted to wear pink tutus like his sister, so he did. Parents commented on this! Now men can wear pink shirts but we STILL get the stereotypical clothes and toys for children in shops. I like to think that this is changing for the better but I fear, from my current experiences in a nursery school, that we may have a long way to go. The media and merchandise do not challenge the stereotypes. Though, I see a glimmer of hope in the "Me Too" movement.

Not being able to have children for ten years and my experiences living in Africa certainly influenced my resilience to being. Barren is a terrible word; so negative, sparse and full of grief. I was desperate to get pregnant in my 30s and was obsessed with my body cycles and women with big bellies. The African women I met in Zimbabwe changed my life - how they loved food and dancing! The obsession with my body, whether fat or thin,

pregnant or slim just disappeared around this time. Maybe it was age, the security of relationship, culture, maturity - I still do not know.

After giving up all hope of having a child, I eventually became pregnant and almost nothing about my body image has mattered since. At nearly 60 though, my body matters to me in ways it has never done in the past. I am grateful for my body and satisfied with it, despite its flaws.

Looking after my 89-year-old mother who is immobile, diabetic, over-weight, riddled with arthritis, in pain and angry with dementia, has put a lot of thoughts about my own body into perspective recently. The old cliché "live every moment 'cos you never know what is round the corner" springs to mind!

This project has caused me to relive some body image memories that I want to share, in case anyone reading this can relate.

- Aged 3 - I had just been bathed at the sink - doorbell rings - I run and answer it naked. The "uncle" at the door made such a fuss, covering his eyes and exclaiming that I should run and tell my mother.

- Primary school - being described as someone "not sporty" but a "good size", so picked last for a rounders game.

- Growing up - comments from adults about my appearance:
  ".... you will be attractive if you keep that flat stomach."
  "If you bite your nails, no one will want to marry you."
  "No wonder you have spots, wearing so much make-up!"
  "Look at those thighs!"

- Uncle stroking my hair and smoothing my stomach, saying I will be attractive one day. "There are two types of girl. The beautiful ones and the plain ones. You are plain but that is a good thing because that means you think about things."

- In my late teens, my body was not my own. I was abused physically and mentally. Nothing terrible but enough to leave scars and influence my future resilience and being. I hated my appearance and struggled to come to terms with how some men can treat women. It was the beginning of my political awareness.

- I became bulimic for a few years though not as severe as the girl I shared a flat with. I went a little off the rails and abused my body because I was sad and had no confidence in my appearance or abilities. My mum was seeing another "uncle" and I had no one to talk to.

Then, I discovered feminism and became aware of strong women.

I slowly took ownership of my body again. I began to read, think, go on marches, throw the bras away, ditch the make-up. This, and meeting someone I felt safe with, changed my life. I was even comfortable on nudist beaches!

Not sure about going nude today! But I am comfortable with my body despite the greying pubes, spider veins, hairy legs, a few wrinkles and the rest! They are part of me.

About the Author

Judith gained a degree in English (1984), then went on to study for a PGCE in Lancaster. She met her partner of over 30 years during this time and they now live near Skipton. Judith has been a primary and music teacher most of her life. Her and her husband spent 2 years in Zimbabwe for V.S.O in 1990, then taught for 2 years in an International School in Malawi. On their return she studied for a master's degree in order to travel again and work for the British Council. In 1998, daughter Sally was born and son Billy came along in the year 2000. Judith and her husband jointly home educated their children and thoroughly enjoyed the experience. She is now a supply teacher.

A Manifesto of Stolen Moments
Roz Weaver, age 28

i. Space

I never knew existence could be so heavy, that loss could mean a weight
pinning me down with a hand around my throat, he squeezes the scream out of my skin
and it stains the ceiling, from where I stare through glazed empty eyes at my floating soul
looking back at a me unrecognisable; that is not me and not my body. The room is shrinking,
imploding in on itself to a black hole and I am plunging deeper into futility
through night terror territory into one-dimensional existence.
The void threatens to swallow me whole but I am too absorbed in life light-years away,
amongst the planets in far off, distant galaxies where I visit dying stars
until gravity has its way. Flung face down on the concrete dirt floor, a year grounded

with spirit split in pieces, until a word tugs gently at the torn hem
of my dress;
it is 'Hope', gazing graciously, wide eyed and innocent,
she offers a carefully folded slip of paper
and I caress the crumpled surface, screwed into a ball tightly
clenched in my fist,
a touch of reality passes in whispers through the pores of my skin,
'til palm unfolds
and pages begin their reverse origami, multiplying blank page after
blank page.
Mine to fill with the words I could not speak, those conceived in
silence, grown in the dark
and birthed by some sacred entity, some Mother Earth
who would not have me give up on this life lightly. The writing
comes in clumps,
forms on the page like poorly fitting clothes, I had not measured
the depth of my feelings
nor the circumference of these curdled thoughts. Their presence
demands
each letter is loved into its lines, that each sentence is scanned for
signs of life
and shown how to breathe on its own. I fill these rooms with
rhymes.

ii. Water

When raindrops escape from the clouds and lick my exposed skin
they taste sadness.
It is why they are always coloured blue or grey, and not pink with
shimmering glitter,
because everyone knows the flavours of sunlight and rainbows and
happiness
without the need for touch, but poetry must be absorbed and drill
deeper than the senses.
It is why I wear shorts in thunderstorms, why each droplet feels
like a kiss;
it's how the words soak in, and it doesn't matter if I sink or swim
because there are still more words on the riverbed floor, carried by
the currents
back to their source, eroded by those who have used them before.

With thirsty lovers
drinking scrambled letters as if hearts were a limited resource. I wash off their scent,
running a bath with the words that stay as I patiently wait for the hot ink to flow
as once it runs cold I know what is lost and grieving has found a new story
and I can move on to the next part of mine. Warm, wet sand between my toes
and I wade into the ocean, the words lapping at my ankles.
I wonder how I was ever afraid of the change in weather, how it took so long
to discover the water cure. I collect the wild, wandering, infant words in my net, tame them,
teach them how to paddle, and when they come across another wild, wandering woman,
drowning as I was, I ask them to let fall their anchor, fill her lungs
with the most delicate creations, keep her afloat, bring her back to land
and show her poetry.

iii. Fire

I have burned your strawberry fields to the ground. These flames taste sweet on my tongue,
dead plants breaking under my bare feet. I have been screaming since that June full moon
but Ceridwen used the twilight to brew me a potion and now a magic curse
runs words through my veins. Did no one teach you that witches don't die at the stake?
We reclaim every cell of our bodies with centuries of words bled onto these pages,
for all the times a woman's voice was hated and her rage was painted as something pretty,
without substance, without solidity, flimsy against the prison cell bars
that restrained our creative spark through history. We strip these silences down to their bones,
rebuild skeletons and hide them in closets 'til least expected,

speaking in the language

of our ancestors' ghosts, our words demand to be unchained from our throats

and now you can't say you didn't hear us say the word no, because its embers

are scorching your sheets. Maybe now the next generation will read that freedom

is more than a concept. When anger melts into soft strokes of calligraphy,

I scribble a passionate prayer that our darkest points

do not brand us with armour nor harden our hearts. These ashes of dead letters

will fertilise new soil, for what are women made for but courage and fires in our bellies.

I will not stop writing 'til I can taste the ripe, delicious, sweetness of a strawberry

without it reminding me of you, and still then my writing will continue.

I will wet my finger, trace directions into the dust, brew courage on the stove,

hand out mugs to every woman who has ever felt the sting of a man's branding iron,

marked by his hands, his skin, his cells.

A woman's creativity cannot be kept in a cage and this collective fury

incites collective change. There may be tigers above and tigers below

but this moment is just one page in a library of feminist action,

I will not water down my reactions. The women before me offer their shoulders to stand on

as I hold fast to the torch that lights the way for the next one.

iv. Air

To me, poetry is oxygen. I don't know how I ever breathed before without it.

The air is enriched, the wind brings ideas and phrases bit by bit

'til they settle on the pen. With words I find freedom, lost in the images

formed in my imagination. Since I was a child

I pretended I could write stories and perform them, copying pages from books
and claiming them as my own creation. After dark, other children
would turn on the television, or creep downstairs for a midnight snack, but my feast
was a dim nightlight and a book of poetry. Reading is my meditation, writing my escapism,
I need them like I need my organs. Inspiration is all around us,
and those who don't feel its breeze don't know what they are missing. We live to create;
whether art, music or words on paper, and I can't surround myself
with hearts and minds whose lungs don't function the same as mine.
Creativity is the purest form of human expression, every inhale is a lesson
and exhale a forgetting, a letting go
of the poison that no longer serves us. I may be miles from ones I love,
ones I hope to see again, ones I have never seen and never loved
but where we share a connection, a swift breath, but still I can tie my words into a parcel
and send them like a hot air balloon across the sky in the hope they touch these others
and envelop them in another temporary reality, for just a short passage of time.
This is what I live for, and the more I get the more I want,
a shamelessly haunting addiction for fact or fiction. I have been in the position
where I wanted to die and a poem by Atticus saved my life. I have been in the position
where one I love tried to end their life and where no one else understood what it felt like,
but hooked up to a ventilator filled with poetry I begin to feel alright.

v. Earth

She both has roots and yet has none that tie her down. She aligns herself with the planets
but stands out from the crowd. She knows there is a past and a

future but lives

here in the now. She calls herself Mother Nature and to her wild wisdom I bow.

Her words connect humanity and speak of love as a verb. Her thunder and lightning

demand to be heard. She uses every season to bloom and to grow, she nurtures plants to flower in spring then kills them off with snow.

She serves the world with stories and rhymes, she passes on tales of old,

whilst we encourage the youngest to fill our shoes and pray their hearts

do not grow cold. She formed me from her blood and soil, she kept me safe with tears,

through the river beneath the river she guides me through my fears. She refuses to stay silent

about the matters of the heart, she names the deepest emotions and turns them into art.

She matches words to the world outside, she gives song to my soul and she empowers

me to speak my senses and leave no shame untold. She translates my mental states,

whether blessing or disease and she welcomes in my demons and makes them feel at ease.

She seeks out what is missing and speaks in prophecy, she understands the universe

and how it takes care of me. Her heartbeat is the purest sound, synced with those who have come before, they teach me how to love my scars

and turn them into words with doors. She encourages me to share of my darkness

and my light because vulnerability is my power and I find this when I write.

Her touch breeds electricity that generates the words, which fall independent

to my hand's direction, I hold the pen for but a turn. Her chemistry breaks down the bonds

to the reality we know, the reaction liberates the words as they burst out and overflow.

She does not intervene with my free will but moves me just the

same,
she knows when to make a rainbow and when I just need rain.
She spurs me on to leave my work out in the world alone
because the words will always visit as this was their first home.
She reminds me of the beauty in this nature's sacred earth
and that I am made from the same fragments so should appreciate
my worth.
She taught me how to speak up and how to project my voice
because words belong to everyone and how I use them is my
choice.
She wants us to change the world one stanza at a time and own our
stories
like they are held to ransom and we are fighting for our lives.
For we are not separate bodies, we are all parts of a whole.
Some may sing, scream, write, paint, dance, or simply listen
but we each have vital roles.
So if your God is a woman, you are both blessed and likewise
cursed,
for we can't ignore the pain and suffering but we can write them
into verse.

About the Author

Roz is a spoken word performer and internationally published poet
living in West Yorkshire, and is studying a Masters in Creative
Writing. She has been published in a number of journals, zines and
anthologies, including most recently with Dear Damsels, Poetica
Review and Token Magazine. Her work has been on exhibit with
London Design Festival, What You Saying, and performed at
Leeds International Festival and Edinburgh Fringe Festival. She is
a recurring guest editor for Printed Words Journal.

Breathe In and Breathe Out, Breathe In and Breathe Out
X Aurora, age 41

When I think about my body image, it's not one carefully constructed thought, how I think and feel is so complex and varied, the thoughts are ever changing, always with me somewhere, and can dominate at the most unexpected times.

It's beyond frustrating as I should know better by now, and I actually do know better, so why can't I have a more positive mind-set towards my own body?

I've spent years trying to find the answer, so that I can be content with who I am, whatever I am, and at any time that I am.

Though now in my early 40s, childless, and about to come out of a 17-year relationship, I fear the worst of my never-ending issues with my body image are yet to come.

'Breathe in and breathe out, breathe in and breathe out. Be grateful for your body, respect your body. Breathe in and breathe out, relax more and relax more. Respect your body, be grateful for your body, every part of your body…' says the deeply soothing recorded voice on a guided meditation I'm following. The instructions are freeing and empowering, being thankful and grateful for every part of my body, reminding me to take good care of it, and to respect it. I can hear the sea in the background, refreshing, invigorating, and yet calming at the same time. I can feel the sun's warm rays gently touching my skin, I'm humbled. In this moment I'm content, I'm grateful, and I'm respectful. The beach has always been my safe place, the place I feel most at peace, the most whole, and the most accepting of myself, but not always of my body.

Predictably out of nowhere my thoughts shift back to the here and now. I'm in my living room, my tranquillity is lost, and I'm now thinking about how many pounds of fat I need to lose to look and feel my best in my many bikinis. How I don't feel toned enough due to suffering a chronic illness which has prevented me from excising for the last 3 years, that I'm slightly older now, how I'm just not in my best shape, so I should hide my body away until I can get back to that. I'm filled with a sense of urgency, but deep down I already know that if I do get my body back to where I think I'll feel good, it still won't be enough for me, I'll always want it to be better. It doesn't matter that I'm a slim petite woman weighing in at 95lbs (I feel at my best at 84 lbs), none of that matters to my critical inner voice. I flit between feeling humbled and grateful to feeling discontented and not good enough in my own eyes. It baffles me as I don't care what other people think, it's what I think that counts, but that's my biggest problem, I'm the worst critic of them all.

The rational side of me knows I place exceptionally high and unattainable standards upon myself for my body. No matter what I see in the mirror I am never content, in my mind I always need to be thinner, taller, prettier, younger, and the list goes on and on depending on the day. When I'm so thin that my ribs are visible through my skin and my face looks sunken and drawn I think I'm fat, and when I put on anywhere between just a few pounds to a full stone I think I'm obese, I always see myself as bigger than I am told I am by those close to me. I know that possibly most of what I see negatively isn't true, and is just my distorted thinking, but I can't seem to change it.

My current thoughts today, that I'm trying to resist at this very moment, are that if I'm unable to have a child, then I have no excuse for not being in perfect shape, and bizarrely that's the trade off, if my body isn't going to go through a pregnancy and child birth, then I have no excuse for not looking my best. Also, despite general aging, the menopause, health issues, and stress all being inevitable factors that will affect how my body looks in time, I'm determined to find a way to evade them. I've spent so many years of unnecessarily fearing what having a baby would superficially do to my body, which is now so insignificant in comparison to dealing with the fact that I may never have the baby I've so badly wanted for so long. I've also just become newly single, at my age, being left by my husband for a woman 19 years younger than him, 17 years younger than me. I know that a lot of men my age are favouring women in their 20s and 30s, so how am I going to compete with them, and most of all win? My inner voice tells me I need to be perfect, look my best, but I never get there as there's always a new best to achieve.

My rational mind knows this is absurd, perfection doesn't exist, and what's considered attractive is so subjective. Not only is it different from person to person, it's different all over the world. Different cultures have so many different and even polar opposite concepts of what constitutes beauty. The body beautiful ideals of mainstream western society are not everyone's aesthetic ideals. But regardless, in every society women are still pressured to conform to a mainstream collective ideal of beauty, whatever that may be within their culture. Our struggles with body image are drastically harming us, whilst heavily lining the pockets of those in the body beautiful business. We all know this, and that being sold endless amounts of products, procedures, regimes, and anything else that will keep us searching for better, for perfection, keeping us trapped in a negative body image cycle that never ends, and knowing this we keep paying up. I have resisted everything except a good face cream so far, but how long until I give up and give in?

I blame my parents, my huge extended family, my peers, and various other people throughout my life for giving me my body insecurities. Amongst many other things, I blame society, the patriarchy, capitalism, racism, but most of all myself for not being able to rid myself of these superficial body issues that really don't matter, but 'oh yes they do' my critical inner voice shouts out like a pantomime villain.

'Breathe in and breathe out, breathe in and breathe out...'

I'm someone who has led an interesting and exciting life, I've had a vast variety of experiences, I have a great career, wonderful personal relationships, and I've definitely had more than a fair share of downs. I really do know that life is about so much more than what our bodies look like on the outside. I've lived this, I know this, I believe this, yet here I am today, still stuck with these negative thoughts about how my body looks.

I'd always been extremely fit and healthy until in recent years where I suffered a chronic physical illness which left me unable to walk, use my limbs at all, or even speak for quite a time. I also endured constant excruciating pain, and many other debilitating chronic symptoms. Thankfully, after spending some time in hospital for treatment and rehabilitation, I have most of my functioning back and am on my way to hopefully making a full recovery. This recent journey with chronic illness has somewhat positively impacted my relationship with my body. At my most ill I rejected the superficial completely, and instead really embraced and valued a healthy functioning body and brain over anything else. I was determined to regain what I could do physically and mentally, and that was what mattered to me the most. As I started to get my health back, it did cross my mind that I wanted to look good at some point too, but at that time it was completely irrelevant. I felt so liberated, I'd finally reached a point of full acceptance of my outward body, I'd got my head straight about what really mattered in life and what really didn't, or so I thought.

The more I recovered and got back into the world, started to rebuild my life and live again, my inner critic began to re-emerge. In hindsight I should've expected this, but at the time it was a gift to see things differently, and I wanted to believe I could hold onto that insight forever, it was one of the silver linings to what I'd been through.

'Breathe in and breathe out, breathe in and breathe out…'

Growing up it was what others had made me believe about myself, right through my childhood and early teenage years, that formed the basis of my body discontentment and led me to eventually becoming my own worst critic.

My parents, though intellectuals, were abusive, and from what I've learned in my adult years, probably psychopaths. They'd sit me down and tell me long tales of how I could never be found attractive or loved, and one by one would go through everything from the tiniest details of what they thought was wrong with me physically and as a person. I believed it all, agreeing with them about the whole load of plastic surgery I would need to be visibly presentable and acceptable. That I belonged to a bizarre subspecies of appearance, and that I would have to exist alone on the fringes of everyone else's world.

Looking back at old pictures it's scary how untrue what they told me was, they were very unwell mentally, and although I know that now it's hard to completely eradicate what they implanted in me, and not be over critical or find things wrong that probably aren't. Especially as there is no wrong, we're all different in our own amazing ways, and we all need to find a way to believe that. I'm nowhere near there yet, but I'm trying.

At the same time others inadvertently helped my parents cause, from my beauty obsessed extended family constantly picking at and critiquing every aspect of how I looked. Or other adults and my peers having an issue with my light olive skin tone, my dark eyes, my dark hair, and constantly telling me that due to this I could never be considered attractive, and suggesting various ways to become white with ideally blue eyes and blonde hair. The funniest was in primary school where some of my classmates suggested I eat white bread to become white like them. Everybody had some issue with my skin, hair, and eye colour, my height, my weight, and so much more. One critic after another telling me how I should look, and what I should do to attain that.

Though my visible ethnicity did trouble me as a child, once I reached my teens this became the main thing I've always since liked about my appearance, and something I really value about myself as a person. So why can't I erase my other body issues that were given to me, and why am I creating new ones for myself now?

I have had a past period of fully accepting my body in my early teens to my early 20's. After another round of abuse from my parents pushing me to tears, and that enraging them even more as usual, and them telling me how horribly ugly I looked when I cried and that it made them want to smash my face in, for the first time ever I managed to escape and make it to a mirror. What I saw in front of me was beyond shocking, after what I'd believed for years, what I saw in the mirror was just normal me, but with tears. My face hadn't contorted and twisted into what I'd been told it did. I was 14, and for the first time it dawned on me that nothing they had ever told me in relation to my body was true. It was like I'd flipped a switch, I instantly accepted myself right there and then. I looked in the mirror and said to myself 'you're not the best, you're not the worst, and you're ok.' In recent years I've amended this to 'There is no best, there is no worst, we're all different, and that's what beauty is' as I don't believe a best or worst exists, and I hate the concept anyway. I suppose at 14 it helped that I wasn't influenced by mainstream culture, and was into lots of alternative kinds of music and culture which allowed and accepted so many different looks and body types, that I didn't feel I needed to conform to anything. It was a liberating time; I'd achieved freedom from those who had chipped and chipped away at my body confidence over the years. I'd realised that people's perceptions of me were tied in with their own perceptions of what society had brainwashed them into thinking constituted beauty, which changes over time as trends do, and their own insecurities and distorted thoughts about their own bodies. Also, for some it was simply about having power and control over others, or their own lives.

So, after all that how did I get back here? Well in my early 20s I started working in TV and fashion, and as you can imagine that was that. I was gradually reeled back into body image negativity hell, something that was rife in everyone around me, both women and men. Also, at the same time society was rapidly becoming more and more obsessed with a naturally unachievable body type, something that today is so far out of control it's beyond scary. I'm not sure how we get back from this, but I know that we have to for the longer-term wellbeing of all humanity.

The truth I know from experience is that we are loved for our inner selves, for the person we are. Our packaging will always change and keep changing as we go through life. Sometimes we'll accept it, other times we'll despise it, and everything else in between. I know this truth, yet my packaging still matters to me. I really struggle to accept compliments about my body if they don't match up with my own opinion of how I look, and I can easily disregard a negative comment about my appearance from someone else if that doesn't match up with my own thoughts. So, if I won't let others put me down, then why do I allow myself to do it all the time?

Well, I've decided right now in this moment, that I have to stop. If I've been content with my body before, then I want to at least try to be again. The tricky part is how, but I'm starting with the obvious of focusing on what I do like, easier said than done I know. I've also given myself two words I like which I'm trying to implant in place of all the negative ones. I'm implanting exotic and unique, as I like what together they conjure up for me, and the word perfect is rendered useless as it's just not relevant anymore.

So, I repeat exotic and unique, exotic and unique as I start a brand-new chapter in my life, and a new journey to hopefully a more positive relationship with my body. I have to at least try right? Yes, we all do.

'Breathe in and breathe out, breathe in and breathe out. Be grateful for your body, respect your body. Breathe in and breathe out, relax more and relax more. Respect your body, be grateful for your body, every part of your body.'

About the Author

X Aurora is an actor, writer, producer, and director working with theatre, broadcasting, film, and conceptual art. She likes to combine her creative and performance work with tackling issues such as climate, racial and social justice, women's issues, and physical and mental wellbeing. Her background is primarily in TV and Radio as a broadcast journalist, producer, and director in many areas including news, arts, and drama. X Aurora has recently returned to the working world after a chronic physical illness forced her to take some years out. She strongly believes in peace and love, fun and laughter, following your passions and living life your own way.

Interlude 3: Accepting that your Body Changes

You have probably taken a biology class that has highlighted the fluctuations a body will undergo throughout its various life stages. So, it may sound laughably obvious when I say:

Your body is **allowed** *to change.*

But sometimes you've just got to hear it.

A change in your body is usually promoted as a negative development. If we were taught to like the new lines in our faces, we wouldn't be sold anti-aging serums. If we were taught to like our love-handles, we wouldn't be sold body-shaping underwear. If we were taught to like new stretch marks across our thighs, we wouldn't be sold preventative creams. This project is here to remind you that change is normal and doesn't have to be feared.

The COVID-19 pandemic has brought fear of change to the forefront of body image discussion. To adhere to social distancing rules, and in some cases, total self-isolation, has meant changes to eating and exercise routines. Especially for those predisposed to troubles concerning control around their body, this can be significantly anxiety inducing.

But I hope it has also served as a reminder that sometimes your circumstances are bigger than your control over your body, as important as that may feel to you. Your body is often feeling its own way, doing what it needs to when adapting to the conditions it finds itself in. Whether this be a global pandemic, experiencing a period of grief, work stress, recovery from an operation – these aren't situations to obsess over change and punish yourself for it. Instead, they are opportunities to notice it, understand why it is happening, and nurture your body through it.

One of the driving forces behind The Resilience of Being was to recognise how body image problems can affect people of all ages. There is still the lingering assumption that the window of 13-30 years old are the only people suffering with body image issues. Young people go through puberty, surrounded by peers who will all be experiencing it differently, immersed in hormones. This grows into young adulthood, time of experimentation and further development of coping behaviours. Succumbing to body image peer pressure and ideals seen in wider society are not uncommon issues in these circumstances.

However, acknowledging this seems to come hand-in-hand with the less accurate assumption that 30+ year olds are miraculously cured of body struggles, simply because they're out of that period of developmental uncertainty.

The post-30-year-old window seems to be more geared towards a pressure to maintain bodies and prevent natural change.

Showing our age seems to be a taboo with the availability of skin tightening products, Botox, or dismissal of grey or balding hair. This is not to say that those who like to take advantage of these products shouldn't feel able to do so, or are in the wrong. It is instead to eradicate the idea that those who *don't* make these modifications 'are not putting enough effort in' or 'letting themselves go.'

People in their 30s+ shouldn't feel like they need to strive to have the bodies they had in their 20s. New mothers shouldn't have a ticking clock in the back of their heads wondering how long they have until they need to 'bounce back,' and new fathers shouldn't fear the 'dad-bod.' It is not your worldly purpose to maintain a body from a different era of your life.

Accepting your body for what it can do and what it has been through is part of a wider rebellion against the shame we put each other through. Whether it be aging, scarring, pregnancy, menopause, weight fluctuation, or just your body shifting around now and again - much like a lot of elements in your life, your body is never going to be permanent. Have a little trust in your body and stop making yourself feel awful when it is, in fact, just doing what it needs to do.

WHEREVER YOU ARE AT ON YOUR JOURNEY

YOU ARE ENOUGH

In Praise of Duffle Coats
Eva Tutchell, age 78

In 1960 I was only the second woman in Britain to have a breast reduction operation.

Before that, I hid inside duffle coats in the winter and carefully tailored dresses in the summer. How I hated my huge breasts! I am small - five feet - and at the age of 16 had a 24" waist, 36" hips and 38G 'bust'. I always looked as if I could topple over at any minute.

Sifting through photos of myself as a teenager in the 1950s I can see how rapidly my shape changed after my fifteenth birthday, so that by the age of sixteen I looked much older than my years. Although I always had a pretty face, all I was conscious of were those unsightly protuberances which preceded me wherever I went.

And they were heavy too. Firmly strapped in, so that I wouldn't wobble, I felt trussed up and so envied the girls in my class with their size 32" A cups, some even resorting to 'falsies'. After gym lessons they stripped off, unashamed, in the communal shower and walked around without caring who saw them. I would cover myself in a towel and sidle into the shower with my back turned, trying to wash without moving and hurrying out as fast as possible in order to get changed before anyone else could see the contraption I wore that passed for a bra.

I was often complimented on the speed with which I got dressed by Miss Samways the P.E teacher – with no discernible breasts and with divided skirts (not shorts) worn over lisle stockings, winter and summer, and who was completely oblivious to my agony.

My parents were Jewish refugees who had escaped Hitler from Slovakia in 1938 and encouraged me to be proud of my heritage. All I wanted was not to be Eva Holzmann but Daphne Dawson, tall with blond hair, captain of hockey, popular with the other girls and above all, flat chested.

Walking down the street, men's eyes would automatically stray to my breasts. Sometimes they looked away in embarrassment, others would wink conspiratorially and yet others would shout out comments. More than once it was "Got the time, Miss? Chest a minute!" I would pretend I hadn't heard and scurry past. But I had and it hurt. At the very few social events I was invited to, boys would be curious but often assumed that my size 38s meant that I was promiscuous and felt affronted when their advances were rejected.

Fortunately, in the late 1950s there were jazz clubs in Soho, where the lights were low and I could get away with a voluminous jumper and dance until the breaks in the music, which I spent in the ladies' lavatory.

The fashions at the time did nothing to help. Tight sweaters pulled in at the waist with waspies, and flared skirts. Worn by Doris Day they had a limited sex appeal, Marilyn Monroe spiced things up with her 'hour-glass' figure but then came the impossibly beautiful but almost androgynous gamine Audrey Hepburn.

And let's not even begin to discuss swimsuits...

I truly believe that the main reason I got into university was because, in my 'A' Level years, I stayed in and studied rather than expose my bosom to the critical world.

My parents tried to understand, but I was a stroppy teenager and tended to rebuff their sympathy.

Then we had a new family doctor. He was young and approachable. My parents persuaded me to see him because they were worried about my mental wellbeing.

He asked me what I was concerned about but I found it hard to put such private feelings into words. Fortunately, my mother came to my rescue and explained that I seemed to have a complex about my breast size. He probed gently, asking questions with great tact and then asked if I would mind taking my bra off behind the screen. I agreed with some reluctance, keeping my eyes closed when he came around to look.

He then uttered words I will never forget.

"You don't have to live like this. There is a new operation called mammary reduction. If you like, I will recommend that you take part in this experiment. And it should be on the NHS."

A few weeks later the news came through that he had been successful and I was to have the operation at University College Hospital.

By the time my turn came, I was in my first term at university – always wrapped in the ubiquitous duffle coat. I was in some trepidation but determined to try anything. The only other person in the ward was a woman in her early 30s who had just had the operation, the pioneer for this procedure, still bandaged up and waiting to see whether it had been successful.

I remember coming around; apparently it had been a lengthy process lasting four hours. I held my breath when the bandages came off. I looked down and all I could see at first were lots of black stitches, considerable bruising and somewhat strange looking nipples, half the size they used to be. But joy oh joy! So were my breasts. It hurt when the stitches came out, particularly the final ones. "We're going to go all the way down the home front today", said the brisk ward Sister. Ouch!

But it had worked. I threw away those wretched constructions that had faithfully been holding me up for three years. I've often thought that the German word for bra - 'bustenhalter' - rather described what those contraptions were like. Not the dainty, lacy things displayed in lingerie departments.

I will never forget triumphantly going to Marks and Spencer to buy my first off-the-peg bra. 36B. I still get a thrill even now nearly 60 years later buying underwear.

I was told that because the operation necessitated cutting through the milk glands I would not be able to breast feed but nothing could dent my delight.

My only problem was that I had told my then boyfriend, who came from Sheffield, that I had gone into hospital to have my tonsils out.

He looked at me rather quizzically and, after a pause, said:
"Well, all I can say is you people down south keep your tonsils in funny places!"

About the Author

Before becoming a full-time writer, Eva's working life was spent in education: first as a secondary school teacher and then as a local authority gender advisor, promoting equal opportunities for girls and boys in schools. During this time, she published guidance for schools and colleges on disordered eating.

Previous publications also include *Dolls and Dungarees: Gender issues in the Primary School Curriculum*. More recently, with co –author John Edmonds, Eva has published two books about women in society – *Man Made: Why so few women are in positions of power* and *The Stalled Revolution: Is Equality for Women an impossible Dream?*

Beyond the Pale
Sarah Boatwright, age 34

I tell her he got me a sun lounger for my birthday.

She snorts. It is a snort that communicates: "what the fuck are you going to do with a sun lounger?"

If she'd asked, I'd have told her that I like being outside on bright days, how it gives me energy and relaxes me all at once. That I want to put my feet up and read a book in comfort.

She assumes I want a tan.

On the paleness scale I can be placed somewhere between cadaverous and spectral; closest shade of make-up either 'ivory' or 'porcelain' (both of them still too orange for my liking).

To be clear, you wouldn't describe me as an elegant, timeless alabaster and I'm certainly no peaches and cream...

Indeed, my own skin tone has been brought to my attention by various people, and on many occasions. It's been labelled as practically 'transparent' by people who know me. A perfect stranger has yelled, 'It is summer, you know!' as he cycled past, on his merry way to wherever. And not forgetting the time my (ex) boss once held up a sheet of paper to my face.

As if the point needed illustrating.

These observations and insults smarted—as they were intended to—and were cruel reminders that my appearance is not the social norm; nothing to be desired, nothing to aspire to.

I brooded upon why I was considered unacceptable and why

these people (all of them white) thought it was acceptable to brazenly point this out to me.

I am an anachronism. The chase for the annual holiday tan has developed into a desire for a year-round healthy glow: its glamorous, slimming and camouflaging qualities a boost for confidence, a sure-fire way to look better in pictures, to fit in.

A tan has become the new normal and by contrast this makes me abnormal in my natural state. Odd, non-conformist. Who would want to be this pale? Certainly, in my case, I am the perfect canvas for a latticework of bluish-purple veins, dark sprouting hairs and blemishes. Illuminated in all their glory.

So, my difference is varyingly seen as either an act of defiance or ignorance, something which a certain type of person feels compelled to challenge, call out, exploit for a cheap joke. To be pale is to be weak; better to show off your sunburn with pride than to deny the sun was ever there at all.

Sometimes I think I am an unwelcome reminder that underneath, others may look a little like me too. It is no wonder this should bring some discomfort, when great effort is made to adopt the look of the Med (though accent pinpoints North Sea).

At other times, I see people visibly gain confidence by my mere presence. They are an inch taller, simply delighted at not being me. Maybe this should make me sad or alert me into action, but I generally alternate between feelings of indifference or martyrdom. Taking one for the team. Letting the bronzed folk have their day in the sun. You're welcome.

I return to work after a week's holiday—which shifts me along one place on the blinding-whiteness scale: think sun-kissed cadaver—and am swiftly judged to be a failure.

My 'progress' is compared with that of a colleague who is back from the Canaries. He is mahogany; the top of his head gleams like a polished bowling ball. I like to think that he sat on his balcony for the duration, rising only for the occasional toilet break or more drinks. That was his holiday and mine was different.

But that is not acceptable. It is not enough. I failed at holiday. (For the record, I didn't really fail - I actually had an epiphany in a state of deep relaxation on the beach, which inspired me to crack on and get a new job. Ha!)

Despite these experiences, I have not ever been sufficiently shamed or compelled into changing. I did not flee into Boots to

Ronseal myself into acceptance, and there was no way on earth I would be bullied into using a sunbed. There is an honesty in my stubbornness. A refusal to deny who I am.

So if, like me, you are off-the-charts pale, consider embracing it. Perhaps you already have. Well done you! Here's what I've learned, anyhow:

- You will save time, money, possibly even your own body, just by leaving it alone.

- Careful in the sun. Good friends will help with shade and sunglasses, should you forget.

- Learn the colours that suit you. In my experience, a lot of muted tones wash me out, and too-bright colours end up wearing me.

- Dressing in head-to-toe black is a bold choice, but will thrillingly make you feel beatnik-ninja-goth.

- You will get looks on the beach, in the pool, in the spa. Try a very bold swimming outfit and an even bolder lipstick.

- While we're on lipstick - it can bring you back from the dead. Be very careful, though. The right shade will sing and pop; the wrong shade and you will look crazed.

- If you are so pale as to practically disappear anyway—and assuming you're not looking for attention—try paring down make-up to the absolute minimum/doing without it altogether. It's quite liberating.

- If you do make an effort when you go out, don't be surprised if people call you 'striking'. This is because you will stand out by your difference. It's a rather special compliment. Enjoy it.

In another less-than-successful conversation with the sun lounger-snorter, I'd tried helping her place a famously pale actress by describing her as having 'luminous skin'. This made her snort too. Like it was a ridiculous thing for me to have said.

I didn't think it was so ridiculous. I still don't.

Anyway, I got a sun lounger. Because he knew I wanted a sun lounger, because he knew it would bring me joy. And it does.

About the Author

Sarah is unmarried, childless and has a job which pays okay. All of this is fine. She tries not to feel guilty about her aimlessness in a society that wants her to want more. She can work hard; she can be lazy. She polarises with her aloofness (bad) and empathy (good, always good). She'd like you to know you are worth more than your looks, your productivity, your material acquisitions. These are not the things people will miss about you when you are gone.
This is her first published work and may well be her last.

A Life of Fluctuation
Jan Willingham, Age 66

There I was, walking down the main shopping street of Liverpool on a cold, dismal Saturday when I caught sight of myself in a shop window. If I tell you that I then went straight to the nearest (posh) department store and bought blusher and other make-up, you'll get a sense of my reaction to seeing my reflection. In that window, I saw a drab, dull and boring person, and I hated it. This was in the 1980s and the event was just one in my on/off relationship with my adult body image.

I say 'adult' for the above as there were a few incidents from my teenage years that have stayed with me. I came into those teen years just as Twiggy was reaching the height of her fame. I was her build with equally skinny body and legs, and a short, blunt-cut hairstyle, quite similar to how she wore her hair. The only difference was that I had inherited the Tripp family boobs and these were definitely not like Twiggy's. My mum, her sister and several cousins were all 'well-endowed' and I had joined the club. To me they felt enormous and I remember feeling acutely embarrassed by them. I used to cringe if I had to pass a building site or any group of males and would try to get past as quickly as possible before I would be spotted and the inevitable 'Hey, Twiggy, where are you going?' would ring out.

I did not spend all my time cowering. There were some good feelings about myself in those growing-up years where I think I was

111

quite confident in my appearance and what I chose to wear, often taking great pride in making my own clothes and wearing some quirky outfits. This was despite still being very shy in my personality. I particularly remember a pair of red velvet bell-bottom trousers I conjured out of my mum's defunct curtains. I really thought I was the bee's knees in those. I think it probably helped that I was one of a group of six very close friends at school, that self-image was not a major factor in our lives, or indeed in the lives of many 'ordinary' people; if there were any trends around, for example, 'Flower Power', we all had one suitable outfit and wore that to death to all the decidedly innocent parties our wider group hosted. There were, however, some disasters as well – the trendy op-art dress which I had badgered my mum to get for me when I was thirteen but then felt far too self-conscious to wear; the time of hot-pants (those little legs!), the school hat, and so on. Away from the group, I did not like attention being focused on me but my self-consciousness then was more to do with poor social skills than a continuously poor body image.

College years were much the same though when I reflect more carefully, I think I was beginning to be more aware of how I looked to others. I was pretty keen to maintain the attention of a certain person (readers, I married him!) and, being surrounded by lots of new people who looked 'different', I remember moments when I was envious of how they looked. I can still picture them in my mind with the 'right' clothes, the 'right' hair, the 'right' everything, and an air of ease about themselves. Lack of money still meant that the one going-out outfit regime operated but at least it was a different one each college year thanks to parental help. I do wonder now though, why on earth did I put a blonde rinse on my hair during my second year? Who was that for, as it really didn't suit me?

I am now in my seventh decade and would love to be able to say that a positive body image is now alive and kicking but strictly speaking that wouldn't be true. We continue to have a fluctuating relationship. I still hate my teeth, my legs and my boobs, and as I've got older, I have added to the list. I am often told by others that they wish they were slim like me but if I point out my dissatisfaction with my still skinny legs or my tum that is as big as my bum in profile, it is dismissed despite these being real bugbears of mine. I am still catching sight of myself in mirrors though in addition to the 'dull and drab' of my 20s and 30s I have added 'Oh my God, who is that old-looking person?' On the other hand, I don't believe that I dwell endlessly on such 'imperfections' as this might suggest. It is more 'moments' of critical appraisal. I have rosacea, my hair is thinner than it used to be (thanks, menopause), cellulite on my arms and legs, and varicose veins now, to name but a few pauses for thought. While I try to keep the first under control with medication and have concluded that unless I need to for health reasons, I am unlikely to do anything about the latter. I am aware of thinking more and more that as I can't see them unless I'm staring in a mirror or performing a contortion of my head and neck, then they are not a problem. If anyone else catches sight of them and thinks any negative thoughts, well, that is their problem! I may not have totally purged the odd niggle or two about these parts of my body but I am starting to learn to shrug my shoulders – oh, and buy good-fitting bras and good foundation. I often go without make-up unless I'm going to the hairdresser's – those mirrors are unforgiving; I love having extremely short hair because it is easy to look after as well as suiting me; I do not have any big beauty routine; comfort is a huge factor when buying jeans and shoes; I am quite happy working outdoors in muddy clothes and a baseball cap; all of which might indicate that I'm not so bothered about my appearance after all. But an invitation to some event or other will arrive and I'll then be fretting about not having the 'right' thing to wear and checking vigilantly that I'm not looking like mutton dressed as lamb when I appear in public!

I am sure I am not alone in saying that I view some other women with some envy, though I think 'envy' may be too strong a word for the actual feeling. The fashion and beauty companies benefit from women (and now, increasingly, men) experiencing such feelings of dissatisfaction with their physical selves; some would say they are adept in manipulating people about their looks, making use of all forms of media. Should we all decide to be happy with how we look, the same industries might find themselves not as profitable. It's not just the young either who get targeted – we older women are always being shown how not to look our age (why do we buy into that?); our teeth, false or otherwise, need to be whiter; we MUST get rid of wrinkles – too late for me as the map of my life is already very clearly laid out on my face; and God forbid that we have any grey in our hair. Though on that last point, I think the manufacturers have cottoned onto the fact that there is a whole new market out there for the 'right' shade of grey for women and men over a certain age!

Thus, it was ever so. I remember my mum talking about how she and her friends during the 1930s and 40s would seek to emulate their favourite film stars in their hairstyles and the odd bit of 'fashion' they could afford. Classical literature also demonstrates that for centuries both sexes have been subject to the same desire to be noted by others for their 'fine' physical appearance. Jane Austen's descriptions of the 'season' in Bath in her novels, the life of Beau Brummell in Regency England, an arbiter of men's fashion of the time, William Shakespeare's 'The apparel often proclaims the man' are all testament to this. In the past only the rich could pay attention to this desire but as the 20th and now the 21st centuries have progressed, and the emergence and importance of social media has come to the fore, business in 'looks' has boomed. Everything – make-up, hair extensions and colouring, fillers, surgery, Botox etc. - is available to and affordable for so many more people to be able to create the appearance that they desire.

Writing this has caused me to look more closely at my feelings concerning my own physical appearance. Certain areas of my body feature so strongly in my image of myself and yet to other people they are not important. On some occasions when I buy an article of clothing, I am aware that I think about others' opinions as well as my own. Why are so many of us so self-critical about our appearance? People seem to be seeking perfection but who is it for? Is it for ourselves, to make us feel good because by wearing the latest fashions and being beautifully groomed we feel somehow better than others? Is it for the benefit of others, to be able to conform to a certain image so we can belong to a particular group, a form of tribalism so we will be recognised and accepted by others like us? Interestingly, not many of my friends like my hair when it is very short, perhaps because it's so different to how the majority of them wear theirs. Is the way we present our physical selves akin to   life in the natural world, just to attract and then keep, a mate? And who gets to say what the image should be? I feel really sorry for the young girls who play around with their faces to emulate so-called celebrities, famous just because they are famous, as these girls can end up looking quite, well, for want of a better word, 'plastic'. Isn't it sad that our focus is so much on ensuring that people judge us based on our outward appearance and not on who we are, our values and beliefs, the intimate person behind all the clothes and make-up? Going around one of the many 'Homes' fairs recently, I was pounced on by a young woman who wanted to show me how to make my eyebrows 'look better'. Before I could say no, she had placed a plastic cut-out of the perfect brow shape on my face, dipped her brush in some powder and applied it over the template. She then proceeded to brush a foundation powder over my face 'to tone down the red'. I gave an honest opinion of how I looked after she had finished which I don't think went down well. To me, I looked as though I was questioning everything with my now much darker, strangely shaped eyebrows and my face appeared to have been dipped in brown paint! In other words, it was not who I am. Love me, love my imperfect eyebrows!

Where does that leave me? Well, I am still fluctuating, still unsure at times, and still admiring other women who seem to be getting it right. I want to look and feel good in what I am wearing according to the circumstances I'm in. It helps my confidence. But I also know realistically that I do not have to be perfect on the outside, and equally, I am realising more and more, that unless my body image starts to massively impinge on me, life is too short to actually worry that my arms are not smooth or that my varicose veins make one leg appear a slightly different colour to the other. As my mother used to say, as long as I'm tidy and my hair is brushed, and I have clean knickers on in case of an accident, I'm good to go!

About the Author

Jan Willingham is 66 (you can decide if it's years, stones or inches - yes, she still doesn't think metrically). She's on a second career i.e. retirement, and wonders how she had time to work. She loves to read, walk in the countryside, craft, bake, dance (even to adverts), eat, drink wine, watch films, and see family and friends but not necessarily in that order. This is her first go at writing: great fun! Her relationship with her own body image continues to fluctuate, and she guesses it always will but such is life.

You Are Not Your Size
Linda M. Crate, age 33

I've always struggled with my body image. Ever since I was a child and up until the present day I have been saddled with the word "fat". Although my friends will yell at me on the days I feel defeated and call myself that.

I always felt like fat was the worst thing a person could be. It seemed like a curse word. It stung. It was the wasp that sought me out just for existing so it could sting me over and over and over again. My tears and pain were never enough; it would always come back for more.

I would look at the magazines and I never saw a girl that looked like me. They were all tall and leggy or petite and thin, but none of them had any discernible curves or cellulite anywhere.

I started feeding into the idea that I was fat and because I was fat that I was disgusting and nothing more than trash. I hated myself so much. I just wanted to cease existing.

When I was in junior high, I remember these boys watching me eat, and they laughed when they saw it made me uncomfortable. For a few months afterward all I would order was zebra cakes and iced tea at lunch (until I saw the damage it was doing to my hair).

Then I always got salad bar and I prayed no one would watch me eat.

I got scolded by my mother for being a closet eater at home, but honestly, I didn't want anyone watching me eat. (I still don't.) I wasn't okay unless we were all eating dinner out or at the house. I just remembered the laughter of those boys and it made me uncomfortable with the fact that I even had to eat. Although everyone did, my brain wouldn't be rational about it.

It took me years and years before I finally accepted myself and my weight. I may not be as thin as I would like to be, but I am going to love every curve and every pound as I am because my weight doesn't define my worth or the person I am.

I am loving, caring, and a good listener. I genuinely and sincerely care about my friends even the ones who decide to blow me off for whatever reason. I try to do the right thing and make the right decisions in order to help not only myself but others. I know sometimes I miss the mark, but none of us are perfect, and I always do my best to make it up to people when I hurt them.

I may not be a size 2, 4, or even 6. But I think it is important to love our bodies and ourselves regardless of where we want to be.

I have since learned from my teenage days that most models in magazines are photoshopped despite how pretty and thin they already are, many people starve themselves to death and have eating disorders that kill them in the modelling industry. I did a paper on it in college and it's heart-breaking to see how many people die trying to be the perfect fit, and no matter how skinny they are their brains convince them that it's not enough.

Yet bigger girls get told to exercise or to put down the hoho, and she becomes the brunt of every joke. I get it, you think my weight is something that somehow concerns you because you see I exist. Well, it doesn't.

How do you not know someone exercises or if they have a medical issue that makes it impossible for them to lose a lot of weight? How do you know what they eat isn't healthy? Why just assume the absolute worst of people you don't even know?

Instead of tearing someone down you could always build them up for the positives you see in their lives and their bodies.

Not every body is the same. We all have different metabolisms, body structures, and some people have medical conditions that make it quite hard to lose weight. So, the next time you think to insult someone maybe look in the mirror and consider that your appearance isn't perfect and no one is defined by their size or lack there-of.

People are already their own worst critics so I think it's important to be kind to people no matter what, and it is important to be kind to yourself. There are days where I still look in the mirror and see an ogre. But I am working on being better at loving myself and accepting myself as I am.

I feel like part of the reason I judge myself so strongly is I see how society views heavier people, and it's not something I want to face. I don't feel good about myself when people make their comments or stare.

I was fat-shamed in college once for having a piece of cake. One, singular, piece of cake. Because how dare I treat myself after a stressful week of classes and studying.

I have tried to stop judging myself because I know plenty of people have got me covered in that department. I know people will see me as nothing but my weight or body size and criticise to their heart's content.

I try to be easier on myself. I try to eat better and do better for my body, take longer walks, and try not to eat out of boredom. I try to limit my snack intake so I'm not just eating for the sake of eating.

I may not be a size zero but I can be comfortable in my own skin despite the changes I want to make. I can love myself whilst simultaneously trying to better myself, and so this is what I've chosen to do.

Because a scale can only tell you one thing: your weight. But your worth is not defined by your weight, your beauty is not defined by your weight, your intelligence is not defined by your weight, you are not defined by your weight. It's just something that we all have to monitor and control to the best of our abilities.

But I am done being ashamed of myself. I am beautiful no matter what my weight not simply because of my appearance but because of my heart and soul.

About the Author

Linda M. Crate's works have been published in numerous magazines and anthologies both online and in print. She is the author of six poetry chapbooks, the latest of which is: More Than Bone Music. She's also the author of the novel Phoenix Tears. Recently she has published two full-length poetry collections Vampire Daughter and The Sweetest Blood. She has always been strange and unusual, but she wouldn't have it any other way.

I'm Due a Metamorphosis Next Year
E. E. Hartley, age 24

Welcome to My Brain

I can't explain how many times I've started to write this. Some incarnations have been angry, some drenched in self-pity but all of them went unfinished. It was only when I started to write about it that I realised how complicated my relationship is with my own body. You'd think being the sole inhabitant of it for 24 years would make me fairly knowledgeable but honestly, I've spent most of that time ignoring it. There is that crappy cosmo-esque quote that says we're an entirely different person every five years; I don't take much stock in it but since I was young my relationship with my body has changed drastically from one milestone to another, so I see the logic. In that respect I should explain that for me bodily self-loathing goes hand-in-hand with how I am doing mentally. I take pride in being quite a strong person but when I am down, I don't like to burden people with my own self-doubt and hatred. I think my internalisation breeds negativity, so once I'm unhappy with one thing I'm unhappy with a lot of things. So, keep in mind when I seem like I'm going off on a tangent about being a bad person that I'm getting back to how it affected my body image.

I was an early bloomer. I was 10 when I started my period. I can't remember my parents ever being happy so it was a relief when mum finally kicked him out. I spent the entire next day playing out in the fields and playground with the kids I'd grown up with. It was liberating. I knew that, although she'd kicked him out before, this time was different. Why is this relevant? That day, the liberation and freedom - I was basically feral - that was the last day I was a "child". I went home that evening to find blood in my white and pink flowery knickers. I was suddenly a fatherless woman. There is a theorist that talks about the traumas of female life - birth, sexual maturity, motherhood - I can't remember who it was or exactly what their point was. I just remember the word trauma. It wasn't a terrifying experience; I wasn't confused or scared. I knew what was happening but I don't think any of us know what to expect when it first happens. I was suddenly "a woman now".

That womanhood that was thrust upon me came hand-in-hand with a lot of other trauma. I had curves. I'd gone from a girl to this woman - everyone could tell. That's how it felt anyway, other kids started to notice I was changing and my mum's friends all started talking about me being a young woman. I didn't get what magical change had happened just because one day I started bleeding. How was I any different than I had been the day before – I didn't see any change but apparently one had happened?

My Body

If you were to ask me to describe how I look I would say three things; I have a pretty face, for a chubby lass, and I'm lopsided. Yeah everybody has one foot slightly bigger than the other and one boob bigger than the other but my wonky body doesn't stop there. My shoulders aren't level, neither are my ears (sunglasses sit on my head at a slant). My thumbs are different lengths from years of thumb sucking, which has also caused an overbite and a wonky row of bottom teeth. It's the whole eyebrows being sisters not twins, but instead of eyebrows it's my entire body. These crooked things are fairly normal even hereditary, mum is the same. But for me, they are imperfections. You might not notice them but I know they are there. So, there is the first chink in my armour.

I choose "chubby" for a very specific reason. If you were to know me personally, you'd hear me refer to my chub, I'm not quiet about the fact that I know I'm overweight. Chubby isn't the same as fat. Fat is one of those words that is said and you can feel people recoil. It's venomous. The people who love and care for you wouldn't ever call you fat, just like you wouldn't call them fat. It isn't a word of love even if someone is overweight, carrying a few extra pounds, jolly, bubbly, chunky, big boned, full of life, ample, curvy, cuddly, plump, even thick. Chubby/chub is cute - you would call puppies or a baby chubby in a cutesy little voice. When I use it about myself, I still gets eye rolls and groans from my friends, but my family don't protest. Chink.

You're thinking - but what about pretty - focus on pretty. Yeah, pretty for a chubby lass. I detest the "pretty" thing. People say it to me in a very particular way. "Oh, you're so pretty though." Though? Meaning "…despite your chunky legs, huge boobs and fat arms". Chink. Now some of you are thinking, how was huge boobs not in the plus column? Huge boobs are great, if they're fake. Otherwise this amazing thing called gravity is a cruel mistress and you have the saggy tits of a granny before you're even 20. Chink. Don't get me started on the stretch marks! Although stretch marks takes us nicely onto my next part.

How Other People Talk About My Body

I have a very vivid memory of my older brother talking about stretch marks. I must have been around the age of 10 or 11 because I know I already had stretch marks – the first of many! He was talking about a girl his age, he's three years older than me. We'd been playing out most of the day, it was a small village and we had been exploring – he usually got told to look after me and my younger brother so we didn't get swept away by the river or something. It was the end of the day and we were all going home. I can tell you exactly where we were in my tiny village, I can even have a guess at who heard this conversation. The girl he was talking about had just gone into her house, we continued on home, someone said something about this girl being great or funny or some other compliment. My wonderful brother, in full neg mode, piped in. "Yeah but I wish she would wear tops that covered her stretch marks." At which point, this stellar embodiment of female empowerment in the shape of the only male role model in my life turned to me and said this. "Don't ever do that. They're so unattractive, it's gross." Chink.

Here I would like to interject for just a moment. I'm sure that if I were to tell my brother this story now, he would take it back immediately. The last fifteen years have done plenty for his growth and he couldn't live in the same house as me and get away with this kind of shit now. He is now a wonderful feminist, who knows he has no say in what women should and shouldn't wear. He's probably more disenchanted with our patriarchal society than me.

However, this moment still had a huge effect on me. He isn't to blame for my strained relationship with my body. Brothers often say things that wound you but you know they don't mean it and they love you. Other people who you don't really know and you know don't have any feeling for you, they are awful to you just for the thrill of being more powerful. Kids are mean to each other, that's how I got the moniker "Big Bum Beth". It was created in the summer of 2005 when I was 10 but went through some amazing evolution, it even followed me to high school. Wave hello to "Big Bi Beth". Although those are warped rumours spun from me not being a homophobe and an ally, the bi wasn't the important bit, neither was the bum. It was the Big that got the weight. The people who used that little phrase are the same ones that hurled dazzling compliments like fat bitch my way. Chink.

Now you need to know more about my armour full of chinks. It doesn't take a psychologist to work out that I have some serious defence mechanisms going on. When I was in my early adolescence, I had my growth spurt early so I was taller than all of the girls in my class and a lot of the boys too. So, I was big in more ways than one. On top of that I grew up with brothers so I possessed volume worthy of a world record. Big, loud and, as my mum would say, bolshy. I was in fact a shy, scared little mouse but my defences and moral standing often meant I came across entirely different. I know my friends would argue against this but I think 'bitch' was a fair description. I went out of my way to keep people at a distance, by being scary and mean, until they'd proven themselves to be what I consider a good egg. My judgement in this particular area took some honing, so I've made some bad choices of friends over the years. These friends often got into arguments with one another, with someone else or with me. I would always defend them or, when it turned on me, myself. And I wouldn't do it quietly. With my loud defence often came a mean streak and I would say things that I am now entirely ashamed of. I would upset people because I'm very perceptive of people's insecurities (I think because I spent so much time ignoring my own). They often retaliated in the most obviously wounding way they could think of. Call the fat bitch a fat bitch. Hold up a giant mirror to someone and you're bound to hurt a person that hates themselves, but honestly, I deserved it most of the time.

How That Affected My View of My Body

The thing with armour, it protects you to a point, but it isn't indestructible.

I was brushing my teeth one day, mum was on the loo, I was wearing shorts. She started touching my calf and said I had stretch marks there. Because of what my brother had said, I stopped wearing shorts, skirts, dresses, cropped trousers. If I had to wear them, I would wear tights, the thicker the better. Then I got stretch marks on my thighs, upper arms, and stomach, to join the ones on my calves and boobs and hips. So, I stopped wearing anything without sleeves, I made sure you could never see any skin past my elbow, ankle or neck. I wore hoodies, jeans and oversized t-shirts. I started to pick bland colours, black and grey just so I didn't draw attention to myself.

My friends got boyfriends and started having sex. I didn't even have a drunk kiss with some of the arseholes I was attracted to that I could regret and be ashamed of. In fact, I never had tangible proof that any man found me attractive. That made me believe I was unattractive. If I ever found myself plummeting to the ground of the romance rollercoaster, I would download tinder, talk to a nice guy until he asks to meet me, chicken out and ghost him. My photos showed the pretty face not the fat lass attached. I was too scared and nervous for these digital men to see the catfish life I led because I know my angles. I didn't want to see the looks on their faces when they realise the "curvy, thick" girl they'd been flirting with was a whale.

The only women who represented my body shape in media were jokes, fetishes or fantasists. They were the punch-line, the supporting role, the unhappy marriage not the romance, the starring role, the happily ever after. So, I felt alone. No one else was having the same feelings as me, and if they were, they were a joke.

The chinks became cracks which, left unattended, make armour weak. I think the fatal blow, that rendered my armour entirely useless, was sometime around age 16. I don't know for sure what this fatal blow was but I crumpled entirely under the weight of hatred from my "friends", my own lack of confidence and being so caught up in what other people thought about me. I missed a lot of school that year, I lost a lot of friends – I fell out with them, detached myself from them, pushed them away – I tried my best to check out. What I should have done was move on and do my A-levels somewhere else. Instead I stayed, crippled myself with self-loathing, and made do with friends who took pity on me. I even convinced myself I was in love with one of their boyfriends because he was the only guy who paid me any attention. So, I spent my last years of secondary school avoiding socialising like a normal 18/19 year old, in fear that I would lose the shaky control I'd put on my life, body and mental wellbeing. Don't get me wrong, I went to house parties, I needed something to post on social media for the ever-desired likes. But instead of flirting and drinking I would sit on a sofa and brood over one drink so that I didn't let slip that I fancied a guy who was dating one of my friends, or worse a guy who couldn't have been less interested in me.

This behaviour led to probably the worst stretch of my life. Looking at it now, I was depressed and very good at hiding it. I had friends who I was a chameleon with, I became who they wanted to be friends with. It was exhausting. Pretending to be someone else really changes how you think about yourself – you start to think you aren't as good as any of the characters you play. I wasn't as smart as one, as funny as another, as caring as this one or as confident as that one. That self-loathing was attached to my body as well. I wasn't like the other girls my age, I wasn't going out in skimpy clothes or having sex with a boyfriend I couldn't even attract. I based my self-worth on how I was unlike the people I'd surrounded myself with; so, because I was different and faking all the things they liked about me, I was worthless.

My Body Revolution

So how has my relationship with my body changed? They say

you are a different person every five years. So, I'm due a metamorphosis next year… but how about when I was 20? I was in my second year of university and with the independence of university came a great deal of perspective for me. For the most part the people I spent time with at high school didn't care for me, made obvious by the one-sided relationships I was struggling to cling on to with them. (I will say though that the friend I did keep in touch with after those awful years of school was always the most encouraging and loving of friends, and I wish I had done more to spend time with them then and will be making up for it forever. You know who you are!) So, I made new friends. These new friends, the good old ones and a new wave feminist awakening kick started five years of a growing acceptance of who I am. I wouldn't call it self-love and maybe acceptance is a bit strong sometimes, but it was certainly an end to the self-loathing.

University bred in me a new confidence in myself. I had tutors who believed in me to the point that I started to believe in myself. My friends started a dialogue that had been hitherto entirely taboo: female masturbation! Another bad choice in friends, showed me a topless photo of herself the first time we really hung out. She would talk constantly about her sexual activity, sexual interests, experiments; even about the sex toys she owned, wanted, was using on herself and with men. Although I don't advocate flashing or starting open dialogue about your private sex life with every new person you meet, I would love to live in a world where women aren't shy of sharing their bodies with the world for fear of sexualisation. Reclaim the nipple!

The self-belief, confidence and openness of my peers had an amazing impact on me. I was no longer a wounded knight but a heroic feminist. However, my relationship with my body image was still very damaged, I still wore hoodies and oversized t-shirts. Any progress I had made with my body had been entirely private. The belief and confidence I had was in my mind but that meant the internal negativity had faded and I could focus on eradicating the negativity elsewhere.

My Body Now

Firstly, let me make it plain that all the negative feelings I had about my body haven't miraculously disappeared with this revolution. It is important to me to change my relationship with my body image but it doesn't stop me thinking about what other people think of it. I have days where I sit and cry about how I look and how I think people see me. People have been telling me negative things about my body for years. But recently I've noticed a change in that.

I've been exploring how I can change my behaviour to make myself feel more confident with my body. I won't for a moment say there was a magic switch I flipped but I will give mad props to the Fab Five. Yes, I am laying quite a substantial amount of my body positivity at the feet of Tan France and Jonathan Van Ness, sue me. Queer Eye might not be counselling or working through issues but it made me realise that I wasn't alone. As did a lot of the female writing revolution – don't get me wrong Dawn French and Victoria Wood were amazing women but Geraldine Granger still resorted to chocolate if all else failed her! I'm talking about Fleabag and GameFace, women reclaiming their messy behaviour, trying and sometimes even failing to get to a better place. It's important to know that women are imperfect but that's fine because they are not alone in their imperfection! They can be the starring role, the romance storyline and still the punch-line – look at Rebel Wilson and Melissa McCarthy.

I was dressing to hide the things I hated about myself and it wasn't working. So, I bought a really gorgeous jacket and some cropped tops. I have these amazing high-waisted trousers that are lovingly referred to as my "Beetlejuice trousers" - they have black and white vertical stripes. They are one of the best purchases I have ever made. I started wearing more colour, autumn is coming up and I'm so jazzed about getting to rock my signature palette! It's amazing how much people notice when you're wearing clothes that aren't your usual thing. I get complimented on my outfits all the time now and it's a real boost – especially when you've bought something new that you aren't 100% on and people love it. I have these outrageous platform boots that are two different overlaying floral patterns, they are just loudly obnoxious. I saw them and thought, god those are ugly I want them. I just can't wait to get back into the colder months so I can start building outfits around them again!

With this change in wardrobe came confidence in my body. That confidence has changed lots of things. I have a new job that

I'm boss at, I go out drinking with my friends and enjoy being with them and being myself, amazingly guys have even started flirting with me! The confidence I have in my body shows. My older brother, the stretch mark police, even said the other day that he'd notice how much more I seemed to care about my appearance and how he thought it had changed me for the better – he was drunk, he isn't always that deep.

Now, as I approach the five year switch, I hope the next step of my journey takes me to being ready to share my body with others and to say I love it rather than the loathing I had for it when I was 15 and 20. I want to be wholly confident not just in my identity but my body too, as they are so intricately woven. Maybe I'll go to the gym and not convince myself everyone is staring at me! With every passing year I think I am less concerned with how people perceive me. I hope the next five years brings that full circle so that I see my body as my problem, my domain, and stop considering others people's opinions and gaze when it comes to my body.

My advice to anyone, whether you identify as someone completely different to me or related to every word I typed, be yourself. It's a cliché, I know. But we are told what is bad about us and what we should be so much that it's hard to know what's good about ourselves and what we want to be. I spent years trying to hide and defend myself, wearing black baggy clothes and being unhappy. Now I'm starting to express myself in my clothes, my opinions, who I choose to surround myself with, and what I do. And I'm happy. It seems ridiculous to me that I ever listened to anyone but myself. Start where you are comfortable; I didn't jump from hoodies and men's t-shirts straight to booby cropped tops. Take baby steps, there are things that I still find daunting – my cropped tops are always paired with a high-waisted trouser, I won't have my midriff on show because of the stretch marks on my stomach. I wore a dress to see Rocky Horror and still wore thick black tights (in a heat wave in August – at a Rocky Horror show… most people weren't wearing much). I don't think I'd be shy about talking openly about my sexual dispositions with any of my friends, if anything maybe my openness would inspire them. What is so bad about loving yourself and also loving yourself?

Tell the people around you how much you love them. Did they tell you something outstandingly brave? Do they have a pair of shoes that you adore but know only they can wear? For many people, as well as our internal critique, our own self-image is based on how other people see us; how they describe, compliment, and view us. We know it shouldn't matter but it does. We should be telling each other what the good things are about us because we are far too quick to criticise and condemn others, and to listen to the negative things they have to say about us. So, hey you! Drink plenty of water and tell someone you like their new hair, or their tie, or the top they wore the last time you saw them. Pay it forward and it might just come back to you.

About the Author

E. E. H. lives at home with her mum, brothers and insane dogs. Her early forays into writing included band-fiction about emos falling in love, don't judge. She studied English Literature at Leeds Beckett University; where she learnt to cringe at how bad her teenage musings on love were. Now she daydreams of being a proper writer living in a beautiful and secluded cottage, with plenty of dogs for company. Her real dream is to be a pirate queen, so if anyone knows of a time machines that guarantees success in the Golden Age of Piracy, let her know.

Interlude 4: Feeling Powerful in Your Body

Even if we're working towards self-acceptance and haven't reached that moment of self-love yet, it doesn't mean there won't be moments of power in our bodies. But with power being a concept not easily measured, it can make these moments hard to recognise and value. Particularly if you're comparing others' definitions of power and trying to apply them to how you are feeling.

Power in your body can be confidence. Whether it be waking up feeling great or taking action that you know boosts your self-esteem. Whatever gives you that rush of self-assurance is worth making a note of, so you can do more of it. It doesn't matter if it's keeping it to yourself or letting the world know about it, whether it's productive, superficial or just for fun. I know for me, feeling powerful can range from being able to do one more push-up to putting on a new set of lingerie, so I'm going to continue keeping up with both. If you find your equivalent, embrace it, and make that effort to include it in your day.

Power in your body can be how you choose to use it. Not everyone has had the luxury of having their body to themselves. Being able to dictate what you do with it is an incredible thing. That could be the choice to give birth, the choice not to, be a sex worker, or cover yourself in tattoos. Always wanted to try that

pole-dancing class? Go for it. Prefer to keep your body covered?
Do it. Prefer not to? Cool.

Your body, your business.

Power in your body can be having empathy. Being powerful in
your body doesn't always mean being strong. You don't need to
believe you are flawless to still hold power with your body, nor do
you need to have a constant fearless approach. Being vulnerable
and questioning is a power all on its own as it is having courage
without having a certain outcome.

Chasing Power

Dissatisfaction with your body and wanting to feel powerful in
it can leave you forcing yourself to change it. But it isn't always as
simple as achieving a physical change. Let's use weight loss as an
example. Sometimes, we think hitting a certain number on the scale
will instantly fix how we feel about ourselves. Since that new
number is the goal, once we have crossed that finish line, the
happiness race is completed. This isn't always the reality.

It is often the case that we assign the feelings and ideals that we
are missing to that numeric goal; confidence, how we want to be
treated, how we hold ourselves in public, power. Sometimes, we
can work so hard towards it that the only thing we see with our
goal-oriented blinkers on is that achievement. So much so that
when we reach the target weight, nothing has actually changed but
the physical self.

Without that immediate sense of fulfilment and expected
happiness, we then come to the conclusion that there is still work
to be done. And so, new goals are created. It's not the case for
everyone, but for those who do experience this, it can be a difficult
cycle to let go of.

If you're working on your body in whatever way that may be,
remember to give your mind some care as well. If you notice a
couple of bits and pieces that need working out, then take the time
and attention to do so. Ignoring them to let them stew and disguise

themselves as body image problems isn't helpful to your overall wellbeing. Your body does not need to be a vessel on which you take out other anxieties.

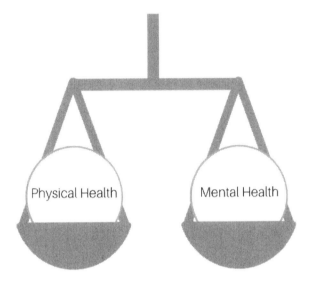

Feeling powerful in yourself isn't just an end result or a reward that you need to deserve, it is something that can always be there, even if it pops up intermittently. Try to notice and value the moments when you feel that empowerment, capturing them to use again and build upon.

Final Thoughts

The following artwork was submitted by 'Amateur Magician,' age 16.

'Amateur Magician' is a young Brazilian artist, whose dream is to work with animation. Having studied art ever since middle school, her work has always been a vehicle to express her ideas and is heavily focused towards storytelling.

> "In this piece, I chose to draw seashells on the sand of a beach as a depiction of body neutrality, and how every single seashell is unique and beautiful in their own way. Just like all humans and their bodies are.

> Upon designing it, I've reclaimed a place that, for as long as I can remember, has represented all the issues I've had with my own body: the beach. Due to the fact that it requires an exposition of people's bodies in a way no other place does, those whose bodies fall outside of what is considered the 'norm' end up suffering a lot there. Not only externally, with the judgmental faces they might encounter from others, but also internally, with their own insecurity. In that way, the beach has, over the time, grown into a 'personal hell' for many."

I wanted to include this artwork to speak to the appreciation of difference and individuality in bodies. As the artist has mentioned, I love the idea of reclaiming a place that is seen as daunting and 'off-limits' for those who feel that their body is not worth occupying that space. Whether it be personal body image struggles or the fear of external commentary, there is always opportunity to open minds to think about body image in a different way, even on the beach.

One of my favourite pastimes at the beach, as a child, was scouring the sand for seashells and collecting them in my plastic bucket. The most difficult part was convincing my parents they were all worth bringing home. The best part was admiring how lovely and unique they all were; why can't we do the same with people?

ABOUT THE EDITOR

Emma Willingham is a 24-year-old creative based in Yorkshire. She currently works in publishing, volunteers as Federation Editor for the NYWF of WIs, and writes mostly for herself. She is keen to be involved in new creative projects and dips her fingers into as many as time can allow her. As Emma's relationship with her body grows and wavers, she is finally starting to understand that she can let it.

www.resilienceofbeing.co.uk

Printed in Great Britain
by Amazon